THE CASE FOR THE
CHOSEN PEOPLE

By the Same Author

MOUNT ZION—THE FIRST HUNDRED YEARS
THE JEWS IN MINNESOTA
THE BOOK OF PROVERBS—A COMMENTARY
JUDAISM AND THE SCIENTIFIC SPIRIT
THE RISE OF REFORM JUDAISM
THE GROWTH OF REFORM JUDAISM
THE CASE FOR THE CHOSEN PEOPLE

THE CASE FOR THE
CHOSEN PEOPLE

W. Gunther Plaut

DOUBLEDAY & COMPANY, INC., GARDEN CITY, NEW YORK, 1965

Library of Congress Catalog Card Number 65–19869
Copyright © 1965 by W. Gunther Plaut
All Rights Reserved
Printed in the United States of America
First Edition

FOR

JUDITH, JONATHAN, AND CAROL

Contents

THE CASE FOR THE
CHOSEN PEOPLE

For faith he gave us land and took the land,
Thinking us exiles of all human kind.
Our name is yet the identity of God
That storms the falling altar of the world.

Karl Shapiro
"The Synagogue"

The Question

For some time now the public has been agitated over the question, What is a Jew? It is an interesting inquiry permitting quite obviously of various answers. Much depends on definitions, much depends on the authority to which the questioner is willing to defer: to the traditional lawbooks of the Jews, to government regulations of the State of Israel, or to popular parlance among non-Jews and Jews. What is a Jew? is essentially a historical and legal query—no more, no less.

But there is another question, far more exciting and far more important. It touches on the raw nerve of Jews and non-Jews alike. It is not, What is a Jew?; rather, it asks, *Why* is a Jew? It deals with existence, survival, meaning. It deals with economics, psychology, politics, facts and fiction, pressure and prejudice—and it deals with theology.

There are those to whom this question is of no interest. Some of them say: Jews are, that is enough. Others say: questions of meaning are irrelevant in a world which is essentially without meaning. Men set their course by the North Star, but that is not the reason for its existence. The French are a nation; their being has no meaning per se, although they may choose to give it content, direction, purpose. And thus, some say, it is with the Jews. They can decide to make their life meaningful, but it is futile to inquire after an extraneous, prior reason for their past and present existence.

This book is directed to those who do find the question important and relevant, and to those others who are willing to keep an open mind in a matter which even to them must present an unusual historic constellation. Of course one can describe Jewish life, Jewish hopes, Jewish law and customs, and all the other elements which produce that fascinating creature called Jew, without any search for meaning. But to do so would leave the picture two-dimensional; the flesh and blood of the subject would be lost in a flat reproduction of facts and descriptions. And so I ask: Why is a Jew?

It is a question not only about Jews but also about Gentiles, not only about the past but also about the present, not only about others but also about me, not only about men but also about God.

CHAPTER I

Impossible History

And History, with all her volumes vast,
Hath but one page.

Byron
Childe Harold's Pilgrimage

Jewish history is a succession of vast improbabilities. It is studded with unlikely heroes, impossible coincidences, enormous failures, and astounding successes. It has received more attention, more literary, historic, and philosophic treatments—to say nothing of theological considerations—than any comparable group in history. Proponents and opponents have described its subjects in extreme terms, reaching from the "chosen of God" to the "devils incarnate." The Jews have been called mankind's greatest blessing by some and mankind's greatest scourge by others. Historians, sociologists, psychologists, political scientists, economists, and philosophers have tried their hands at describing or solving the puzzle of this people's existence, by bringing the story into the purview of some method or theory. In many instances their attempts have proven highly enlightening, but taking Jewish history as a whole, they have, as we will show later, failed dramatically. For these analysts have made one fundamental error: they have attempted to write this history in terms of the probable, the likely, the expected, the normal, when more was to be gained by considering its one really distinguishing element, namely, its abnormality and its improbability.

Let me illustrate what I have in mind by touching briefly on ten highlights of this improbable people's career. They span two thousand years and are chosen because of personal preference and not because of any definitive weight in the balance of impossibilities. By sheer accumulation they produce the strange story of this strange people.

THE UNLIKELY MEMORIES OF IMPROBABLE HEROES

To begin with, the unlikelihood of Israel's peregrinations through history is cast into bold relief by the character of its own folk memory, its own historical and quasi-historical books. Most nations remember their founders as great men and women who were hardly touched by human foibles and commonplace frailties. Where such existed, patriotic or sacred recollection would tend to obscure them. Mohammed's irascibility is now remembered as holy zeal; Napoleon's murder of the Duke of Enghien is now all but forgotten; and Soviet history describes Nikolai Lenin as the flawless apex of human history. When fifty years ago Charles Beard suggested that the fathers of the American revolution may have been moved by considerations other than purely patriotic ones, that perhaps they were influenced by such lowly motivations as money and mercantile advantage, he was bitterly attacked as a destroyer of fundamental American beliefs.

From the very beginning the heroes of the Jewish people experienced a different fate. None of them was remembered primarily as a saint, not even Moses, the greatest of them all. The Bible depicts him as a man with distinct shortcomings and weaknesses: he was physically or psychologically handicapped when speaking in front of others; he was guilty of manslaughter; his marital relations embarrassed his family; and in a crucial moment, when he had to witness to God's unlimited power, he failed his Master at the rock of Meribah. And to make doubly sure that Moses would not be accorded the status of a demigod or even saint, his grave remained unknown. He was buried somewhere in the desert, and no pilgrimages were ever made to any site identified with him.

Even the more shadowy figures of Israel's prehistoric past, Abraham, Isaac, and Jacob, who might well have been surrounded by the transfiguring halo of a remote antiquity, came under the searchlight of the chronicler. He wrote sacred history, yet he managed to be both pious and honest. Twice, when Abraham's personal security was at stake, we are told in disarming detail how the patriarch seemed ready to sacrifice the honor of his wife. (I say, *seemed* ready, because a subsequent tradition attempted to rescue Abraham's honor. Later generations did not always have the courage to tell the story in its original, unlikely fashion.) On one such occasion Abraham told the Egyptians, into whose land he had wandered, that beautiful Sarah was not his wife but his sister—and Pharaoh who apparently had a good eye for pulchritude promptly took her to his private chambers. Had it happened only once, our hero might have been more readily forgiven, but it happened again when a similar situation presented itself in the city of Gerar.[1] There was a shocking flaw in the hero's character, yet he was the archetype, the very progenitor of his people. So important a character fault makes him an unlikely candidate for the position of Founding Father—but then he is only one of many unlikely heroes yet to follow.

His son Isaac, the second of the triumvirate of the heroic patriarchs, is another of these improbable heroes. If the truth must be known, he was really a rather undistinguished person. He did not object when his father prepared to sacrifice him, he allowed himself to be managed by his father's servant who delivered a wife to him, and this Rebecca in turn promptly became his manager. Even the one gift which was truly his own was taken from him, when Jacob with the help of Rebecca surreptitiously obtained the blessing intended for Esau. (Maurice Samuel has written a delightful essay on this subject.[2])

And what are we to say of Jacob whose career begins by stealing his brother's birthright and deceiving his aged and blind father? What he did later to overcome these early shortcomings redounds to his credit, but in the expected heroic story of the Progenitors he does not play his unsullied part. He was a human being like all the rest of Israel's unlikely heroes and that was the trouble with them. National heroes should not really be remembered as fully human.

One could go on and on. Young Joseph was no model child, far from it, and he doubtlessly deserved the cordial dislike that his brothers accorded him. As for his brothers, who became the fathers of the other eleven tribes, they too had character flaws. They were ready to kill their brother and let their poor father mourn for him as one dead. The murderous violence of two of them is recounted in the Bible. One of these was Levi, ancestor of Israel's priests, the guardians of the Temple. How more unlikely can a hero be if his own father says of him:

> Let my soul not come into their council.
> Unto their assembly let my glory not be united.[3]

Besides the down-to-earth humanity of these men one does not even find the mystique one has come to expect of national heroes, ancient and modern. Romans used to connect their invincible valor with the youth of Romulus and Remus, who according to popular legend were suckled by a wolf. The early kings and heroes of Greece were demigods or at least the sons of gods. The divine Baldur and the incomparable Siegfried were the sources of German inspiration. Americans remember with pride the way in which the early pioneers—strong courageous men with sturdy virtuous wives—conquered an obstreperous wilderness and gallantly fought "the deceitful and wicked Indian."

No wonder that a good many Australians consider the ignominious beginnings of their white settlement a source of some embarrassment. After all, who wants to be descended from felons and other undesirables exiled to the antipodes when British jails became overcrowded? Can we be surprised if present-day Germans attempt to play down their immediate dreadful past and consider the constant rehearsal of yesterday's sins injurious to sound national feeling? When I went to school in Germany in the 1920s we learned little about the causes and progress of the war of 1914–18. While all of us knew of its disastrous ending, we were given to understand that Germany did not really lose the war on the field of battle, but was defeated by traitors. In this respect Germans felt and feel like most other people: it is inglorious to be reckoned among the weak and vastly reassuring to be part of a group that in its basic structure is heroic, strong and, in the final accounting, invincible.

On all these counts the Jews score negatively. One of the most competent kings in its history—competent, that is, if measured by the usual historical standards of administrative capacity and organization—was none other than Ahab, husband of the notorious Jezebel. Non-Jewish historians are agreed that he was a great monarch, but Jewish memory as encased in the Bible and preserved in later tradition thinks of him only as a compromiser with idolatry and as the counterfoil to the dynamic and godly Elijah. Other people might admire this kind of king—Jews tried to forget him. In contrast, David could not qualify either as a Jewish Hammurabi or Akhnaton. Yet he, an essentially tragic figure, a mixture of divine sensitivity and human weakness, who commits adultery and murder, becomes the folk hero, the founder of the Messianic Dynasty. His greatness derives from his humanness and not from any heroic stance.

Most crucial of all: Where is the people that will remember servitude as the starting point of its national history and rehearse this fact over and over again? Defenders of the Bible's accuracy have with some justification pointed out that the story of Egyptian slavery is in itself ample proof that the Exodus was an historical fact. No people would invent this kind of past for itself. In Israel's history it is the unlikely that seems to be likely, the improbable that seems to supply the raw material for the actual. If anything, one should have been surprised at a heroic beginning for Israel's history.

Also, the manner in which foreigners are given credit for the spiritual development of the people is a matter of considerable interest. Although a strong and normal chauvinism runs through Israel's literature, there are crucial exceptions which cannot be overlooked. For instance, the fathers of the Bible, in the Book of Ruth, retained the genealogical assertion that Ruth the Moabitess (of a people with whom marital union was strictly forbidden!) was the ancestress of King David, and thereby the ancestress of the Messiah himself. There are all sorts of explanations for the inclusion of this literary idyl in the biblical canon, but the fact remains: David was at least in one part of his ancestry a Moabite. Similarly, Jewish tradition has agreed that the deepest philosophic portion of the Bible was not written by a Jew but by a Gentile. The most ancient Jewish sources already assert that the Book of Job was the work of a non-Jew. Its majestic cadences sprang from the tortured soul of one who was not a son of the Covenant. Or take the most characteristic administrative and judicial institution of ancient Israel, the Sanhedrin. It dates back to none other than Jethro, a Midianite priest, who advised Moses on the administration of his people. It was Jethro, and not a Jew, who was thereby made responsible for the beginnings of democratic government and the organization of justice. Not Moses the Lawgiver stands at the fountainhead of the court system of his people, but a foreigner!

Indeed, it is a strange people, with its improbable heroes enshrined in unlikely memories.

THE ENIGMA OF THE EXODUS

The events surrounding the freeing of the Hebrew slaves from Egypt are so fraught with improbability that one cannot blame those historians who have sought refuge in the only apparent rational conclusion. They hold that the event never could have taken place as described, and therefore in all likelihood never did take place. But too much in Israel's history, both actual and spiritual, depends on, and relates to, this central fact for it to be treated as a pious invention. Every single piece of Israel's literature from its dimmest beginnings on until today is staked on this central circumstance of its birth, the progression from slavery to freedom. Yet it must be admitted that history gives us scant clues about the admissibility of this recollection in the sacred precincts of acknowledged fact.

There are in recorded history numerous instances of enslavement and rebellion, but no historian has been able to record a peaceful liberation. No people ever gave up slaveholding without some desperate external or internal conflict. The Roman system of peonage withstood a few rebellions, such as the one led by Spartacus, and was submerged only in the morass of a decaying empire. A bloody war brought about the official end of American slavery and still failed to produce a liberation worthy of the name.

But an Exodus as it is described in the Bible, a liberation without the application of force, is unheard of elsewhere. My literalistic friends will interject that the succession of ten plagues can hardly be described as the absence of force. True enough, but I am trying at this point to treat the event purely on a non-theological basis. Read the story without the incidence of divine interference, and you have a most implausible tale. The ancient historians already knew as much. They therefore repeated an Egyptian tradition which ascribed to the Hebrews such noxious qualities that the Pharaoh had to let them go to safeguard the health of his country. This fits in neatly with some of the personal prejudices that Tacitus, who repeated the legend,[4] held against the Jews, and it ironically anticipated the "scientific" claims of the Dührings, Fritzsches, Rosenbergs, and their henchmen. American slaveholders of a hundred years ago similarly described their unfortunate chattel with whatever epithets could hide their own iniquitous practice. They called them subhuman, lazy, dirty, but were quite unwilling to give up the obvious economic advantage that free labor bestowed upon their system.

We would have to stretch our imagination considerably to assume that the Egyptians were moved by high and humane considerations in giving freedom to the Israelites. Nowhere do we have a record of Hamite John Browns or Lloyd Garrisons. Some historians connect the Exodus with the retreat or expulsion of the Hyksos, the warlike invaders and erstwhile rulers of Egypt who centuries before had come from Asia Minor and in whose train the Habiru (believed by some to have been the prehistoric Hebrews) may have descended into the land of the Nile. Other writers posit certain internal economic conditions in Egypt. Still others relate the fate of Israel to Pharaoh Akhnaton, believing the Exodus to have been in fact a forced expulsion

which followed the reversal and failure of Akhnaton's religious reforms.

But if we remain with the bare and essential facts of the
story as told in the Bible—and the more we learn from archaeological and other historic finds, the more we learn also
to respect the essential accuracy of the biblical stories—we
remain face to face with an event of high historical improbability. Seen as a singular event it would doubtless submit to some reasonable explanation, but seen as a pivotal
happening in Israel's genesis and measured against similar
events in other peoples' histories it takes on the mantle of
that enigma which seems to be endemic to the story of this
imponderable people. Moreover, it is but one such event in
a meandering stream of continuing questions.

THE RIDDLE OF SINAI

"Moses received the Torah at Sinai"—so runs one of the
basic teachings of tradition. Most modern scholars, both
Jewish and non-Jewish, have cast serious doubts on the assumption that the Torah (the Pentateuch or Five Books of
Moses) was indeed created and conveyed in this way. The
dating of the various parts of the Torah is, however, in
dispute. Estimates vary from a time preceding Moses down
to the fourth pre-Christian century. But with very few exceptions scholars agree that the place called Sinai cannot
be shorn of its central position in this drama of law creating, lawgiving, and law acceptance. Something fundamental happened there. Disagreement exists over the nature
and extent of the happening.

The location of Sinai as an individual mountain is also
in doubt. Perhaps it was a mountain range, perhaps it was
the name for an area in the peninsula which divides Egypt
from Canaan. But more significantly, the term Sinai really
stands for a series of events, ranging over a considerable

period of time. The Bible describes it as forty years. Whether one is a biblical fundamentalist or a critical scholar, one is bound to accept the fact that the essential memory of the Jewish people correctly recollects a series of events during which *a whole people*, whatever its size, *placed itself and its future under the guidance of an invisible God and His law*. Yet, judged by an ordinary scale of historical predictability, it was highly unlikely that this would ever take place.

Of the two propositions, namely, the acceptance of an invisible God and the acceptance of a specific moral law, the former offends less against the laws of probability. True, there was no precedent to placing oneself in the hands of a divinity that could not be portrayed visually, but this may have been a tribal tradition among the children of Abraham, Isaac, and Jacob, a tradition which they preserved throughout their years of slavery. Moses helped them to refine it, but in all likelihood he did not create it. An old Jewish legend has it that Moses was doubtful from the very first that the signs and wonders which he was bidden to perform would convince his people of the genuineness of his message. After all, the Egyptian magicians could and would equal his feats. Whereupon the legend has God say to him: "It is not what you will *show* to them, but what you will *say* to them, which will convince them. For therein will they recognize the ancient tradition and promises handed down from Jacob, Isaac and Abraham."[5]

But could a mass acceptance of even the rudimentary elements of the Torah have been possible or feasible for the children of Israel? Judging by their economic and political circumstances, they must have been a generally uneducated and illiterate folk. We know how slavery debases the slave. In an age in which literacy and culture were the privilege of only the very few, even among the ruling nations, how much more abject must have been the lot of those who vegetated at the bottom of the social heap! Jewish tradition says that throughout their enslavement the Hebrews maintained their own language, but language is not culture, and nothing in their past history could have possibly prepared them to accept a law which in its major moral imperatives ran counter to almost everything which experience and knowledge would have suggested.

The Bible itself, to be sure, indicates that the generation which left Egypt was not ready for freedom and its demands, and therefore had to perish in the desert. Still, to believe in the acceptance by that and succeeding generations of a substantial part of the law and its spirit is to test once again one's imagination and the bonds of believability. For quite apart from the detailed laws themselves, their spirit and goal stretched far beyond the nationalist experience of any group. Nothing in the past of Israel could have prepared them to renounce for all foreseeable time the exploits of temporal power. Canaan was to be conquered, but only as a space for living, not as a base for political and military expansion. It was to be the locale for the execution of the nation's real purpose, namely, to be "a kingdom of priests and a holy nation." Is there a nation today, more than three thousand years later, which with all the moral, spiritual, and intellectual teachings that men have since made their possession, willing to announce similar goals and to incorporate them in its constitution? Hardly. Times are not yet ripe for such a massive declaration, and if they are not ripe today, how could it have been possible then?

THE BARREN PROMISED LAND

The matter becomes more mystifying when we take a good look at the Promised Land the people were to occupy. The Bible repeatedly refers to it as a land of milk and honey, but historians and geographers are generally agreed that this was either a view from the desert or a fond recollection in later days. The land had its lowlands of fertility, especially along the coastal Plain of Sharon and the Valley of Jezreel. It may have been amply wooded in those days; but the south, the Negev, was neither then nor later a blooming garden, and its annual rainfall was probably not substantially different from what it is today. Modern Israeli farmers still experience enormous difficulties in coping with the vagaries of nature, and it may safely be assumed that their ancient forebears fared no better. In this respect Canaan certainly could not compare with fertile Egypt or with the Mesopotamian breadbasket. It was a land of beauty, to be sure, with its contrasts of mountains and valleys, with the sea and the desert, the rivers and the luminous quality of the sky—but the day-to-day sustenance it would offer was relatively undistinguished and looked like "milk and honey" only as one viewed it from the arid desert.

If the natural resources of the land lent it an average desirability, its function as a bridge between east and west, that is, between Mesopotamia and Egypt, vitiated what few advantages it had. Living in Canaan was literally living on the highway between antiquity's major Near Eastern civilizations. One of the roads which led through its southern part and then up the eastern side of the Jordan was known in ancient days as "The King's Highway." An alternate route ran along the Mediterranean shore through Gaza and Jaffa to Carmel and Tyre. Up and down these roads marched the largest armies of the time. Throughout most of the centuries that the descendants of Abraham occupied this little land, it was an object of military contention, the battleground of foreign armies, or the passageway for conquering troops. Devastation, pillage, and rapine were the normal results of its geographic situation; insecurity and instability, its psychological and political consequences. Besides, the land was so small as to offer no escape from unwanted visitors. It is a bare thirty miles from Jordan to the sea, and one hundred and fifty miles from Dan to Beersheba. Jerusalem's chief attraction lay in its potential as a fortress, its high and rocky eminence promising some surcease from the ravages of constant conquest.

It was not necessarily improbable that a people could sustain itself in some measure even under these circumstances. The ability of man to conquer the adversities of existence is surprisingly great. What does seem improbable is that in such surroundings, on this trampled-down bridge of antiquity, this highway and battlefield of centuries, anything permanent should have been able to grow; that this arid bridge would be the birthplace of poets and prophets, historians and philosophers; that this unlikely place would be the locale for and origin of the world's greatest spiritual revolutions. It had none of the protective features of Greek mountains and harbors, of Byzantium's favored site, of Britain's splendid isolation. Its promise was war, and devastation its all too frequent fulfillment.

Today, with modern Israel's growing industrial civilization aided by mechanized farming, some of the scars of the land's age-old wounds are beginning to fade. Only thirty years ago a visitor would have found them still much in evidence. One still could see, as it were, the armies fighting at Megiddo and the troops marching on Gaza. Even the new mantle of love and the warm verdure of spring which had begun to envelop the land could not quite hide the old nakedness of this little land bridge, crying out into the unbelieving ears of man its defiant assertion: "I am the Promised Land!" Its barren rocks made its past history seem an almost arrogant improbability. It seemed so then and it still seems so today.

THE HOLY ACCUSERS

The next improbability has to do with that strange breed of preachers and literateurs known as the Prophets. The English word, derived from the Greek "to foretell," reflects only a portion of the Hebrew term *navee*. The *navee* was the announcer of God, he was His foil and His tool, he was an often unwilling servant driven by a demand that could not be resisted. The message that welled up within him was so overpoweringly clear that its divine source seemed beyond doubt. For him to say "Thus saith the Lord" was to state the already obvious. "The Lord hath spoken," said Amos, "who can but prophesy?"[6]

But such prophecies are in themselves not the seat of improbability. Other peoples, other climes, other nations, other times have known prophets and seers, announcers and interpreters of the divine will. What set the Hebrew prophets apart was that they presented a unique combination of national conscience and universal address. Amos preached universal social justice, not merely Jewish social justice, yet he brought this universal message to the only audience he knew, his people, his nation with whose fate and future he was desperately concerned. When Isaiah foresaw the time when all men, not just Jews, would beat their swords into plowshares and their spears into pruning hooks, his immediate message was addressed to king and court and to the people of *his* nation, to whom peace and war were urgent questions demanding decisions of *Realpolitik*. The combination of the parochial and the universal, the national and the supranational, constituted the framework of the rostrum from which they spoke. This framework was unique, yet not in any sense improbable. But the conclusion the prophets drew from this set of references *was* improbable, and especially so since the nation whom they served enshrined their message in a holy canon.

The improbable element consists of a single thread that runs through all their prophecies, poems, warnings, threats, and sermons, their exhortations and their imprecations: the cause of Israel's likely or actual disasters, present, past, or future, *is Israel itself*—not her enemies, not forces outside her borders, not some caprice of the divine, nor a war of the angels. The main responsibility lies not even (with some exceptions) in the corruption of politicians, princes and merchants; rather, it lies, always and forever, with the whole people, whether poor or rich, educated or uneducated, innocent or not so innocent. A war is lost not because of the superiority of the opposing forces, but because of one's own moral inferiority. The beleaguered Israelite city falls not because of hunger or treason (we have already referred to this as the favorite excuse of the Germans after 1918), but because social inequity had sapped the strength of the community and thereby rendered it unable to defend itself properly.

One may say that this was a clever rationalization. It exculpated failing generals and defenders and put the final blame either on God or on that amorphous and anonymous mass "the people."

But the prophets were not rationalizers, quite the opposite. And the really improbable aspect of this whole thought process was the adoption of its conclusions as a basis for national self-esteem. When indescribable sufferings came upon Israel the prophetic message was castigation first and only then, comfort. The nation accepted as its national literature a series of books which publicly proclaimed its many failures as a sure proof of its unworthiness in the eyes of God.

THE GREEK CONUNDRUM

The sixth improbability lies in the relationship between Hellenism and Judaism. A hundred years after the death of Alexander, that is, toward the end of the third pre-Christian century, Greek speech, literature, philosophy, and habits were becoming dominant factors in the lives of most Mediterranean peoples. This was true even in Rome. Its military expansion failed to overcome the influence of Greek civilization; on the contrary, hundreds of years later when the Roman empire reached from the Atlantic to the Indian Ocean and *pax Romana* was supported on the double points of the sword and the law, Rome itself had surrendered its gods and its soul to the pervasive force of the Greeks. Everywhere did men of culture and thought embrace the beauty and the insight, the sophistication and the enjoyment of Attic civilization.

Palestine was no exception. But here as nowhere else, the embrace did not betoken love and the union did not signify marriage. It was a temporary acculturation to the ruling power of the Greek Seleucids. Their Jewish supporters, mostly drawn from the upper classes, became bilingual, adopted Greek dress and customs, and added baths and gymnasia to the diversions of the rich. The common people remained apart, their loyalty to ancestral faith and custom unimpaired. When assimilation became the planned policy of the state, as it did under Antiochus Epiphanes IV toward the middle of the second century, the country erupted into savage internecine and national warfare.

Yet it is not in armed resistance that the improbability resides, nor in the fact that the small and intrepid band of rebels should long withstand the unequal battle against a mighty empire. It is the aftermath which constitutes the unlikely. Once the battle was won, one would have expected the pristine culture of the descendants of Abraham, Isaac, and Jacob, the heritage of Ezra and Nehemiah, to have vigorously rooted out all vestiges of Greek culture, which after all had been the embodiment of the enemy. This did not take place. In the moment of victory this people evinced a strange syncretizing ability, which it had shown before, but never so clearly: to transform the gifts of a foreign tradition into something essentially new. Judaism found itself, then and thereafter, not in slavish adherence to a national purism but in its conscious and successful adaptation of foreign and often opposite elements. Here was born the idea of the creation of a definitive book, a canon whose thought was both simple and complex, whose sources, though diverse, were transmuted into the spirit of this people. Into this anthology or Bible now were gathered not only the books of Moses and his successors, but also the wisdom of Greek-oriented teachers!

The indigenous national message of an Amos and the story of Elijah the folk hero stand side by side with the sophistication of an Ecclesiastes, the philosophy of a Job, and the Proverbs of an unknown teacher of Hellenic bent. In the moment of triumph this people turned its back on the available fruits of victory. It could now proceed to build its future purely on its past. In the hour of bloodstained triumph, a time least likely for compromise, Israel having reaffirmed its singular tenacity to the tradition of its fathers chose to say Yes to the world around it.

THE RAMSHACKLE PLACE

The next improbability relates to the story of a "dead" man who was alive. Tradition has it that shortly before the conquest and destruction of Jerusalem and its Temple in the post-Christian year 70, a procession of mourners filed out of the beleaguered city. In those days even the enemy ac-

corded last honors to the deceased, which is more than
would be done today under similar circumstances. Instead
of heading for the valley of Hinnom, where the burial sites
were, the procession made its way straight into the camp of
the Romans. It turned out that the coffin bore no dead man,
but the very much alive scholar and popular leader Johanan
ben Zakkai. Brought before the commanding general, the
future Emperor Vespasian, Johanan sought and obtained
permission to establish and maintain an academy in the village of Yavne, after the inevitable and foreseeable conquest
of the land by the Romans.[7]

The story has certain prophetic or miraculous overtones,
and in fact it may be doubted whether the event ever did
take place. It is not the story of Johanan's coffin which
elicits wonder, but rather the actual consequences of the establishment of the little school in Yavne which were quite
real and historical. For if anyone should have been dead
and ready for honorable burial it was Judaism and the Jewish people after the utter destruction of the Temple and the
devastation of the land. With one stroke, the two apparently
essential aspects of Jewish survival were destroyed, namely,
the state with all its trappings and the traditional worship
practices of the people. The coffin of Judaism was ready for
burial. But the improbable occurred, the dead man was
alive, and if at first not vigorously, then at least sufficiently
to allow him to gather strength for dealing with an even
greater national disaster: the ultimate dispersion of the
Jewish people, which was to happen only two generations
later. Meanwhile, the Jewish people made the unlikely shift
from Temple worship to Synagogue worship, from sacrifice
to prayer, from priestly guidance to rabbinic leadership—
and managed to get along without the state altogether.

It all sounds very simple now, almost two thousand years
after the event. "Prayer became a substitute for sacrifice"—
this may appear the most natural and expected culmination

of previous history, but little in that history would lead one to expect this shift and its successful realization.

The synagogue had been slow to develop. It had its origins during the first dispersion in Babylon. It grew out of informal assemblies and study sessions held in people's homes. It never was meant to be in competition with the established services in the Temple, with its priestly tasks and sacrificial ritual, which formed part of Israel's spiritual constitution. Non-priestly Israelites who had some knowledge of the Jewish tradition would interpret the scriptures and keep alive among their fellow exiles a sense of commitment to the lasting values of Judaism. When the people returned to their homeland, these little houses of assembly were soon to be found in many communities. Their influence was at first limited and secondary. Certain prayer practices and prayer formulas developed, but they were at the periphery, not the center of religious life. Jerusalem was the head and the Temple the heart of ancient Judaism and when the heart was torn from the body and the head severed the patient should have died. Yavne provided the unlikely seedbed of survival.

An academy at Yavne—what a pretentious term for a one-room effort! Yet from this room with its handful of students eventually grew a fantastic system of schools and universities that spread all over the world. From it developed the utterly revolutionary concept that study and the development of the mind in the service of God could be an aspect of religious practice. "Learning as religion"—the transition was made while the state died and the people were prostrate. It came about not by government fiat. It arose out of the inner recesses of an improbable people, who until then had been torn by a factionalism so bitter that a later tradition was moved to say: Jerusalem was destroyed because of civil discord.[8]

There was every reason for Titus (who succeeded his father Vespasian as general) to report of his victory: "Judea is

conquered, she is no more." Even if he had known the Jewish people better, he would probably have said the same
thing. As it was, he was undoubtedly the victim of many of
the misconceptions, superstitions, and rumors which circu-
lated among the nations of antiquity about this strange people. For instance, a highly disturbing feature of Jewish
life was the observance of the Sabbath. As a revolutionary
social measure it has no equal in all the history of man, and
not surprisingly it earned for the Jews no accolades, but only
a reputation for laziness. Who had ever heard of a full day's
rest every week, when it was well known that, with the exception of special holy days, man was meant to work every
day of his life? Or perhaps it was the fact that this institution applied to slaves as well as free men which made the
Jews suspect. But then, the Jews had other laws about servants and slaves that contrary to most traditions, ancient
and modern, treated such people as human beings with
rights that were divine in origin and not privileges on human
sufferance.

But more than anything else it was the idea of a statueless
invisible God that was especially disquieting to the ancients,
so much so that even a historian like Tacitus was moved to
write:

Moses, in order to implant himself more securely in the future
of his nation, instituted new rites which were in contrast to those
of all other mortals. Everything we revere is despised by the
Jews; per contra, all that is impure with us is permitted by them.
The image of an animal (an ass who had shown them the way
to an oasis in the desert) is adored in their Temple. . . .[9]

Legend has it that when Titus conquered the Temple, he ap-
proached the Holy of Holies and, fully expecting some living creature to be hidden behind the sacred curtain, thrust
his sword through it, thereby meaning to kill the spirit of
Judaism.

Whether or not this story of Titus is historical is of little significance. Symbolically, by destroying the Temple, he did thrust a sword through the curtain and reveal that indeed there was no physical God which it hid. The universal God who had chosen Jerusalem as His dwelling place, Jerusalem the holy, Jerusalem the magnificent, a place worthy even for an invisible God, now found His abode in ruins. To remain Israel's God, He would have to make another start, as it were, in a ramshackle place, in an unknown village—an unlikely beginning in an improbable setting.

THE ENDS OF THE EARTH

The destruction of the Temple and of the vestiges of statehood took place in the year 70, but the total dispersion that resulted in what we today call the Diaspora had to await another rebellion. This happened two generations later when the miseries of war and devastation were no longer remembered and when new Messianic expectations swept both the masses and the intelligentsia. Bar Cochba (Son of a Star) convinced many, and probably himself also, that he was chosen by God to liberate his sorely stricken people. But not only were the ravages of the earlier war repeated, they were far exceeded by Emperor Hadrian, who resolved to make an end of this obstreperous nation. Those who escaped the slaughter were sold into slavery, others fled and only a relatively small portion of the people, among them men who managed to hide their devotion to the Torah, were permitted to remain in the land. The Diaspora had started in earnest and a new pattern of survival developed, a pattern which would last well into the modern age.

Wherever possible, Jews already living in the major Mediterranean communities redeemed their brethren, and it was not long before there were new Jewish settlements throughout the Roman realm. We do not know whether it was at this time or later that Jews penetrated as far as India and China and established communities there, followed the source of the Nile into the heart of Africa and left their traces in the languages and cultures of nations who were not to be rediscovered by white men until recent years.[10] From then on until the re-establishment of the Jewish state in 1948, Jews wandered to and lived in every land and every clime. At times, as in the Mesopotamian valley about the year 1000, in Spain shortly thereafter, and in Eastern Europe and America in modern times, the communities became strong and numerous and provided encouragement for their dispersed brethren. At no time, however, did the majority of Jews gather in one land, nor was there any realistic promise of the far-flung dispersion coming to an end.

It is not dispersion, not even individual and communal survival that must be marveled at, rather it is the fact that in all their separation the Jews maintained a common bond and, except for regional differences and linguistic peculiarities, an essentially common culture which developed, changed, and matured across the continents and centuries. This was achieved without any central authority, by the voluntary submission of succeeding generations to the interpretation and guidance of scholars. One would expect great, if not unbridgeable differences between various Jewish communities to spring up. There was much that would distinguish a Jewish courtier in Germany from his contemporary fellow Jew living in a Moroccan *mellah*, but withal, both followed the same basic customs, the same laws, and had the same fundamental outlook on their different existences. Their Jewish philosophy changed, and amazingly changed apace, in various lands. To repeat this fact makes the happening no more likely, especially when one takes into consideration that the concept and the actuality of distance are so different today from what they were then.

It is almost a truism to state that today the people in Viet-

nam and Panama, in Kenya and Siberia, join in the neigh-
borliness of the front page. We can know as much about
them as we choose to know and we can reach them almost
as quickly as we can anyone. It is hard to turn back the
clock of the mind and imagine oneself living in an age in
which one's neighbor was only he who lived next door; in
which travel was restricted to the immediate vicinity; in
which knowledge of other places and other lands, let alone
other continents, was filtered largely through the exaggera-
tions and inaccuracies of oral reports and legendary writings. Traders and occasional travelers were the links between
nations; the average citizen rarely left the narrow confines
of his birthplace. Our contemporary habit of spanning vast
mileages without much thought makes it difficult for us to
appreciate the sense of distance which even Europeans of
the last generation possessed.

My father was a grown man before he traveled farther
than ten miles from the little village in Germany in which
he and his forebears had lived—and this in an age of rail-
roads and in a country which stood high in technological
development. Even later, a journey anywhere assumed the
proportions of a major undertaking. Our family lived in
Berlin after the first World War, and I recall an occasion
when we were to visit Hamburg, which was only a few hours
away by fast train. The preparation for this journey literally
took weeks. Travel for the sake of travel was not part of the
Central European experience. We tend to forget this in our
age of complete dislocation and gigantic migrations.

From the vantage point of a village in Carpathia, the
Jews in England were a lifetime away, to say nothing of
the Jews in North Africa or in Babylon. Yet, they communicated across the improbable waste spaces of time and
distance. They remained one community, obeyed one law,
followed one culture and did so voluntarily. Nothing more
astounded the mediaeval traveler Benjamin of Tudela than

to find Jews in lands he had hardly heard or dreamt of at home, Jews who followed and practiced the Torah of Moses in essentially the same manner as did his own family in Spain.

Some years ago I occupied myself with a study of the Jews in Minnesota. In the course of my research and travels I came across the records of the tiny communities in the distant frozen northlands of the state. No village was so modest that it did not attract at least one or two Jews. Sometimes the communities were large enough to engage a teacher and to establish regular prayer services; more often the small-town Jews were without the comfort of coreligionists. But Jews lived everywhere. How they had wandered there, and how in every part of the world and through twenty centuries they had maintained some vestige of their culture and religion, how they had safeguarded their identity and in most cases their will to be Jews, remains one of the marvels of human persistence: an unlikely people, separate yet one, with an improbable bond reaching down through space and time.

REFUGE OF THE DEVILS

What is one to say of Christianity's relationship with Judaism? One follows the rise of a faith which preached redemption, charity, forbearance, forgiveness, and all the virtues that in common parlance have come to be associated with the term "Christian." Yet, as the centuries rolled by, there grew within this faith a deep and pervasive hatred. It was the hatred of a child for its mother, this hatred of Christianity for Judaism and its people. A single line leads from the Gospels to the Fathers of the Church, from the decrees of succeeding Vatican Councils to oppression and ghettoization and the badge of shame, and finally, though unintentionally, into the pits and ovens of Auschwitz.

The story has been told many times by Christians and by Jews.[11] It speaks of many things. It speaks, for instance, of a good and kindly man, John Chrysostom, whom Cardinal Newman called "a bright and cheerful, gentle soul, a sensitive heart, a temperament open to emotions and impulse; and all this elevated, refined, transformed by the touch of heaven." Such was St. John Chrysostom, yet it was he who in his sermons called the Synagogue "a criminal assembly of Jews, a place of meeting for the assassins of Christ, a house worse than a drinking shop, a den of thieves, a house of ill fame, a dwelling of iniquity, the refuge of devils, a gulf and abyss of perdition. Whatever name more horrible that could be found, will never be worse than the Synagogue deserves."[12]

What he preached was to be repeated ten thousand times over in the centuries to come: ". . . as for me, I hate the Synagogue . . . I hate the Jews for the same reason."[12]

Centuries later another leader of the Church, St. Bernard of Clairvaux, called the Jews an "evil seed," an epithet often invoked. "What is there," he wrote, "in that people which is not crude and coarse, whether we consider their occupations, their inclinations, their understanding, or even their rites with which they worship God. For war was their business, wealth their whole craving, the letter of the Law the only nurture of their bloated minds, and great herds of cattle, bloodily slaughtered, their form of worship."[12]

I read on: of the attempts made throughout the centuries by Christians and Moslems to separate the people of Abraham from the faith of Abraham, herding them into churches that they might listen to sermons aimed at conversion, degrading them, expelling them and killing their children—all in order to coerce the Jews to abandon the Torah as their law and way of life.

"For nineteen dreary centuries," another Christian observer wrote, "their history has been one of almost uninterrupted tragedy. Scattered throughout the world, scorned of all nations, they have been forced to suffer every form of persecution which men have been sufficiently cruel and ingenious to invent. Words fail to depict their suffering. To torture, rob and exile them, the despotism of a hundred kings has been exhausted. . . . By a refinement of torture Jewish children under fourteen years of age were taken from their parents . . . to be brought up as Christians, so that, in their madness, Hebrew mothers would sometimes murder their own offspring and then commit suicide."[13]

Where force prevailed not, bribery was sometimes resorted to. In Poland converts to Christianity were offered a title to nobility and a sum of money. This too was of no avail. Perhaps Hitler, in his perverted mania, realized what generations of his predecessors had but dimly perceived, namely, that the task the Church had set itself was an impossible one. To him it was apparent that the only solution lay in physical extermination.

Historians will argue forever about what produced the special brand of virulent anti-Semitism which characterized the rise and fall of the Third Reich. I say, the fall as well as the rise. For it is now established that Hitler's special anti-Semitic insanity hastened the ultimate decline of Nazism. With all transportation facilities strained to the utmost, with manpower needs at the point of desperation, with the survival of his armies and the existence of the Reich itself at stake, Hitler insisted that the extermination of the Jews had to go on even at the cost of defeat itself.[14] The gas ovens were the Nazis' last line of defense, the killing of Jews their last act of defiance. It was as if they were driven by a fate beyond their ken, by a need deeply imbedded in the blood stream of history. From Matthew to Origen, from Chrysostom to Bernard, from the yellow badge to our time, runs a tortuous line which degenerated into spiritual and, later, racial desperation. Hitler was certainly not in the Christian tradition, but the prejudices which he exploited were.

It is not the proliferation and persistence of hatred that arouse my wonder. Jews generally read this tale neither in wonder nor in anger, only with sorrow, though no longer with the resignation that once characterized their fathers and that, to the disturbance of many, accompanied them even into the gas chambers. We are past all this now. Informally the third session of the second Ecumenical Council has acknowledged the Christian guilt, the black books have been written and collected; few read them, even Jews want to look away. I will not quarrel with them. They have been dulled to pain and they want to raise their children as normal human beings.

But there is a sense of wonder which I feel to the roots of my being: wonder at my people, how they survived, how they persisted, how they said yes when the whole world shouted no, and no when yes seemed to be proof of faith. For if persecution, hatred and malice are the dark side of Jewish history, there is also the bright and shining side that speaks of faith, endurance, hope, and intrepidity and made it possible to live in the hovels of degradation, to wear the yellow star, to be wanderers over the face of the earth, to be struck without striking back, and to sing even in the moment of death, "I believe that my Redeemer cometh, and though He tarry, yet will I believe."

This "yet will I believe" is the refrain of the impossible, it is the unexplained, the inexplicable marvel. At this I wonder.

This "and yet" is more than the animal's need to survive. For Jews usually had a choice; there was an escape for them except in the days of the Nazis. Not to have taken this choice, not to have escaped, and instead to have preserved their identity in the face of tortures and blandishments, was,

humanly speaking, impossible. If the black side of the coin
has its sheen of implausibility, its bright side tells a story
that makes no less a demand on our credulity.

THE DREAM OF ISRAEL

In May of 1948 the State of Israel constituted itself as
an independent commonwealth. It is easy enough to write
it down. Yet of all the unlikely events in the Jew's long history, this is perhaps the most improbable, the least predictable.

Of course, one can have recourse to the explanation that
this is what Jews had ardently and unchangingly desired,
hoped, and prayed for. But that is merely answering one
riddle with another. How could their hope have been kept
alive as a realistic achievable goal, when all Jewish history
since the expulsion seemed to proclaim failure and defeat?
Or, to put it differently, why should any people continue to
believe in the efficacy of a God who had not helped them
demonstrably, so it would seem, in nearly two thousand
years? For the desire for Palestine was bound up with God's
promise, and a Promised Land undelivered for so long
should have lost its glamor long ago.

If at least it had been a rich, fertile land beckoning the
starved inhabitants of sickness-ridden ghettos; if at least it
had been a prize worth yearning for, a gem which glittered
with beauty! But Palestine was nothing of the kind. For
many centuries it was considered one of the most desolate
areas in the world.

John L. Stoddard, a popular lecturer of his time, traveled
there some ninety years ago and recorded these impressions:
"Neither words nor views can adequately represent the
desolation of this frightful area, seamed with one thousand
sterile gorges. Even the Sahara is less dreary. . . . The
Judean wilderness is a series of absolutely barren and appall-

ing mountains, divided from each other by great chasms, flanked with frowning precipices, as if the country had been gashed and scarred by demons. It would be like a horrible nightmare to think of being lost in these Judean canyons, where every drop of water is drained away, where every vestige of vegetation has vanished, where nothing is available but yellow burning sand and rocks. Birds, beasts and men shun it as if smitten by God."[15]

This was the land of which this strange people dreamed. This was the Holy Land, whose physical condition played little or no part in shaping the national dream. The true essence of Palestine lay not in its physical reality; it reposed in its spiritual nature, it was to be redeemed by God at the end of time. Meanwhile one went there to die, not to live. If a Jew could not reach the land before he breathed his last, he could at least have a small bag of its sacred soil placed in his coffin, so that on Judgment Day he might make the last journey more easily.

Judah Halevi, Jewry's poet laureate of the Middle Ages, epitomized his people's dreams in his poetry and sealed it with his life. Zion, as he sang of it, was not an earthly place; it was the future idealized, the Messiah drawn down into the present with cords of love.

> O Zion, beauty and gladness of the world,
> Thine is all love and grace, and unto thee
> In love and grace are we forever chained.

Jerusalem had a geographical location, to be sure, a latitude and longitude, but its true significance was plumbed in study chambers around the world, where pious students would debate the laws of the future Temple or the calculations of the Jubilee Year, once the return was effected.

Scholars maintained rabbinic academies in Palestine throughout these years. Their numbers were small even though their influence was not. Here lived the master of cabala, the great Isaac Luria, and here lived Joseph Caro, the author of modern Jewry's authoritative lawbook, the *Shulhan Arukh*.[16] For those who traveled here to die, the vagaries and dangers of travel were many. Judah Halevi undertook the journey to crown his ecstatic dreams. Robbers slew him in sight of his beloved Jerusalem.

Twice during the long exile did men arise who would lead the scattered remnants back to the unlikely land of their ancient forebears. One was David Reubeni, the other Sabbatai Zevi.[17] Both aroused in the breasts of the oppressed people the hope that the Messianic days had at last arrived. God had sent them, they proclaimed, to redeem His people. Especially in the case of Sabbatai Zevi the expectations of the multitude rose to fever pitch, before the bubble burst and despair replaced the happy and excited mood of anticipation. The messengers of God turned out to be purveyors of deceit and the Promised Land remained a promise, a pledge to be redeemed at the end of days, for not man but God alone could end the Diaspora. A human reclamation was thought impossible.

Not until the nineteenth century was there any serious discussion of a humanly authored return. It was no accident that the first to foretell the impossible were not Jews but Christians. Truly Orthodox Jews would have no part in forcing the Lord's hand by returning en masse to Palestine, and the new Reformers were universalists to whom Jewish national aspirations were anathema. But even the few Christian voices were advocates only of what *might* be if the impossible turned possible. They were not at first raised in behalf of realistic, achievable plans.

John Stoddard was one of these Christian prophets. In the mid-1870s he wrote:

A man who has no Hebrew blood in his veins may indulge in a dream regarding the future of this extraordinary people.

Suppose the nations of the earth to be assembled in council. . . . Suppose the miserably governed realm of the Sultan to be diminished in size, imagine portions of it to be governed by various European powers, as Egypt is governed by England at the present time. Conceive that those Christian nations moved by magnanimity should say to this race, which they, or their ancestors, have persecuted so long: "Take again the land of your forefathers. We guarantee you its independence and integrity. It is the least we can do for you after all the centuries of misery. All of you will not wish to go thither, but many will. At present Palestine supports only six hundred thousand people, but, with proper cultivation, it can easily maintain two and a half million. You are a people without a country; there is a country without a people. Be united and fulfil the dreams of your own poets and patriarchs, go back—go back to the land of Abraham."[18]

From the vantage point of Stoddard's time it seemed impossible that the return would take place. That it did, three score and ten years afterward, and as he speculated, through the collective resolutions of the nations of the world, is but the current chapter of the unlikely story.

Yet not here does the wonder lie, not in the prophecies nor even in their fulfillment through the consent of nations. The impossible cast of this latest chapter lies in the self-emancipation of a people who rose from the mired swamps of oppression and from the smoking ovens of a dozen death camps, to claim the land not on sufferance, but by right.

One must have a full view of Jewish life in Europe and America toward the middle and end of the last century to appreciate fully the improbable turn of events.

In Eastern Europe Jews were struggling to catch their first glimpse of the modern age. Politically they lived in utter darkness, prone to humiliation and destruction at the slightest whim of an autocrat. One has only to study the writings of the Jewish emancipators, the *maskilim*, to taste the bitter tears of despair they shed in pursuit of near hopeless goals. One must read the manifestoes of Moses Hess and Leon Pinsker to see the gulf that separated hope from fulfillment.[19]

In Western Europe and in America the spiritual soil for a return was equally barren. The cry was for assimilation, for an embrace of Western culture and an abjuration of yesterday's dreams. "America is our Zion and Washington our Jerusalem," wrote Gustav Poznanski. French, English, and German Jews felt the same toward the lands of their allegiance. To the traditional Jew, Palestine was the land of past glory and Messianic promise; other Jews who could no longer believe this proceeded to excise all mention of the Promised Land from their prayer books. One can understand how Arnold Toynbee, unaware of the rich, inner life of Jewry and looking primarily at its outward, political manifestations, should have been led to believe that this people was not truly alive, that it was a fossilized remnant of an ancient civilization incapable of playing a vital part in its own redemption. How could he have pronounced otherwise, judging as he did by ordinary standards of history's progress?

How could anyone have foreseen the bearded prophet from Vienna, Theodor Herzl, who, though himself thoroughly assimilated and westernized, would lead the Eastern masses whom he did not truly understand toward the Promised Land? How could anyone foresee the struggle and the agony, the astounding idealism of the pioneers and the near extinction of the whole people, the conflict of nations, the rivalries and blood baths, the chance of war and the frail suffering of peace—all to conspire toward the recreation of a state that had not been for two millennia? And when it was born at last to the Hosannahs of many former enemies and the sheer disbelief even of the Jew, it was denied its right to be by neighbors who had been friends in centuries past. Israel—the very name declares its troubled destiny: "one who is struggling with God."[20] It was a fateful identity which the state's chosen name proclaimed.

The founders knew that they were participants in more than the routine establishment of yet another new nation, an event to be duplicated dozens of times in the years that followed. In the moment of fulfillment the proud architects of Israel felt themselves "impelled by historic association" and saw themselves as part of a higher dream. In their Declaration of Independence they wrote: "Accordingly we . . . by virtue of the natural and historic right of the Jewish people . . . hereby proclaim the establishment of the Jewish state in Palestine, to be called Israel. The State of Israel . . . will be based on the precepts of liberty, justice and peace taught by the Hebrew prophets. . . ."

Was it a chapter closed or another opened in the story of this unlikely people? Who is to say? We are perhaps too near in time and emotion to grasp its full significance. We can rehearse the circumstances, retell the political and military happenings which led to that day in 1948, but we will not have begun to explain the elusive meaning of it all.

We can speak of other "impossibilities": of the East European *shtetl*, the small town in which culture was the possession of the poor as well as the rich, and not as elsewhere in the world accessible only to the privileged few; or of the explosive quality of Jewish literary, scientific and artistic genius in both East and West, producing in our time an outpouring of intellectual and esthetic creativity far beyond the realm of the likely. We can speak of this and much more: of untold sorrow and indescribable joy, of tears and laughter which resound in heaven. We will merely add other stones to the wall of wailing and of wonders to raise its impossible structure higher into the arch of time. The people of Israel could not have been, but they are—alive, struggling toward an end they do not comprehend, and following a destiny of which they know nothing.

At this above all I wonder, at this people's visible way, but even more, at its elusive Why.

CHAPTER II

The Search for Answers

All history . . . is an inarticulate Bible.

Thomas Carlyle
Latter-Day Pamphlets

Staggering is the number of answers which over the centuries have been presented to solve the riddles of Jewish history. Jews are the best documented, if not always the best understood, people in the world. Perhaps the very plethora of books on the matter reveals that the riddle continues to resist solution.

I will present some of the answers which have been given. They come from various camps—from Jewish tradition, from the Church and the Mosque, from modern Christians and metaphysical historians, from Marxists, psychologists, and Jewish humanists. In this catalogue most of the philosophers of Judaism will be prominent by their absence. For a presentation of their systems far exceeds the limits of this book, which is essentially a personal statement, the non-systematic inquiry of one man, and not a critique of philosophies. Therefore, Maimonides and Judah Halevi, Mendelssohn and Krochmal, Hermann Cohen and Rosenzweig will not be treated here, even though many of their insights have become part of my own outlook. Where I could trace their influence, I have gladly acknowledged it. More often, this was not possible, for who knows with certainty the strands and roots of his own faith?

THE BASIC APPROACHES

Basically, all answers fall into either of two categories: they are either theological or they are not. The theological answers, in one way or another, find that all meaning and manner of Jewish existence are founded ultimately in God's will, that God has had a hand in Jewish fate. The non-theologians will either deny this or leave the matter open. They proceed in their search and description with human tools only; they use the insights of the old-line historians and of new-line psychology; they describe the Jew archaeologically and sociologically, economically and politically. But to them, God has no *objective* part in all of this.

They admit, of course, that God had a *subjective* part in Jewish life. That is to say, Jews (and Christians) may *believe* that He played a dominant role in shaping this people's history, that Jews acted and lived *as if* God was their general. But their subjective faith did not objectively make it so. It is historically true, say these writers, that Jews believed this ancient tradition about the Chosen People, but their belief does not thereby create the fact. The consequences of their belief are historical realities, the content of the belief itself is not. And since historians aim to be as scientific as possible they cannot be expected to let theology influence their work. Private religious convictions about these questions they may have, but these will not be allowed to enter the pages they write.

In a way the theologians have the best of both worlds. They know the reasons for Jewish existence and they also can, and do, use all the findings of the non-theologians. There are many books on the How of being a Jew that are replete with modern scholarship. But if the author is a committed believer in the role of God, then he will not be able or willing to disguise this belief. Somewhere it will shine through.

Having said this and having divided the two camps, I must quickly admit that this book is no exception. It takes a definite position. The reason for having written on this subject is the most usual and at the same time the most compelling: the author's desire to share his point of view with the reader.

MY FATHERS' ANSWER

My ancestors had great trouble staying alive, but they had no trouble at all explaining why they managed to do so. It was God's will if they lived and God's will if they died. To them it was obvious that He had willed Israel's existence. The Bible says so in many places. The expressions vary, the sense is the same:

The house of Israel is My people, saith the Lord . . .

They are the seed blessed of the Lord . . .

For the vineyard of the Lord is the house of Israel . . .

The Jews are called God's elect, His messengers, His witnesses. God chose them to be "a kingdom of priests and a holy nation."[1]

Why did He choose them? This, my ancestors averred, is divine mystery. Already in Abraham the future election was foreshadowed. He was promised that in him and his descendants all the nations of the earth would some day be blessed. The covenant at Sinai and all that followed was God's fulfillment of the ancient promise.

But my forefathers went even further back. An ancient legend tells that prior to the actual creation of the world God so arranged the natural order that at a given moment in history the waters of the Red Sea would part and let

His chosen ones pass to safety. In other words, to the ancient Jews and to many generations of their descendants down to our day it appeared that Israel's special God-relationship was built into the very structure of the universe.[2] There are not many Jews today who would care to phrase it this way, but there are a goodly number among us who answer the Why of Jewish existence simply by referring to the Book of Books, which contains the Answer of Answers. It is written that He chose this role for us. That is enough. It is not a role filled with earthly privilege. On the contrary, suffering is the badge of choice.

No wonder, said the Rabbis of old, that no other nation wanted the yoke of Torah, the burden of God's service, although the opportunity was offered to all. The Bible does not say so, but Jewish folk tradition, in its interpretive collection called Midrash, spins out these thoughts in great detail.

Other legends speak of the Torah being revealed simultaneously in the seventy languages of man; and an old interpretation remarks that the Torah was given in the desert for the desert was accessible to all men and belonged to none. For the same reason the Torah was revealed openly, in the sight of all men, and not secretly to a few.[3]

The How of Jewish life was the natural (or shall we say, supernatural) consequence of the Why. What the Jew had to do was laid down by Bible and later tradition, which was called oral tradition, because not until the second post-Christian century was it committed to writing. Both Bible and oral law were considered the word of God, the latter being taken as the divinely authorized expansion of the former. There were many commandments to carry out—but then, what greater privilege could a man enjoy? It all centered on one goal, the service of God; and it all was related to the eternal, immovable Why of Jewish life, the choice and the will of the Eternal One.

What did it matter if the privilege was bathed in tears? This too was God's will, just punishment for our sins. When they are expiated, as they will be in time, the Messiah will come, Jerusalem will shine in new splendor, and "on that day the Lord shall be One and His name be One."

This traditional attitude was developed and refined, but essentially it remained the same across the millennia. The How of Jewish life changed sometimes slowly and sometimes precipitously; the Why remained the same. Orthodox Jews continued to adhere to this ancient belief and so do many Conservative and Reform Jews, although they might put it differently, in more up-to-date language and more sophisticated terminology. In the classic prayer book of one of the most radical Reform congregations, one finds a meditation containing these sentiments:

Behold! The Temple's mighty edifice crumbles, the columns break asunder which bear its dome, for Thy hand, O God, has dashed them in pieces, Thine arms have shattered them and torn down the walls of Jerusalem. . . . And once more they returned to the place of Thy Temple to build it anew, Thy right hand again took them up and dispersed them over the whole globe, as far away as the sun casts its rays. . . . Marvellous are Thy ways, O God; incomprehensible are the decrees of Thy wisdom.[4]

The prayer was written by Samuel Holdheim during the 1840s, the same Holdheim who in most other matters eschewed traditional theology and traditional practice.[5] In this respect his answer to the Why of Jewish history was the answer of the past, and on the whole this point of view continues strongly among my people. In one way or another the old theological *raison d'être* still exists for the Jew; in fact, I suspect that it exists for most Jews, at least in some vague fashion. Somehow they feel that a God in whom they only half-heartedly believe and to whom they often render little more than lip service has still something

to do with their lives. We might call these latter-day descendants of the prophets "theologians by intuition"—still,
they stand where my fathers stood, although with less conviction.

I must add that there are other Jews, many of them
ardent believers, who will have no part of such an approach
to the Why of Jewish existence. They consider it outmoded, anachronistic, and downright uncivilized to continue to hold such doctrines as election, choice, and God-
approved suffering. We will come to these dissidents in
good time. In contrast, most Christians still are in the
camp of old theological approaches, and it is well to see
how the Church has dealt and deals with the riddle of the
Jew.

THE ANSWER OF CHURCH AND MOSQUE

Jesus was a Jew reared on the Bible. Christianity refers
for validation to the promises and prophecies of the Bible,
that is, to the Bible as Jesus knew it, the Jewish Bible.
(Later, when the Gospels and the other documents that
make up the specifically Christian scriptures were collected,
the new anthology was called New Testament and the
Jewish Bible, Old Testament.) The Old Testament became
the necessary spiritual foundation of the New and thereby
of Christianity. Historically therefore as well as theologically, there could be no Christianity without Judaism; and
since Judaism was coexistent with the Jewish people, the
Jew as a being of special identity had a living relationship
to the Church. He himself might be unaware of it, but the
Church could never be unaware of him. It was a cardinal
point in Christian thinking to consider the Old Testament
as having been fulfilled by the New. Or, as the Church
Fathers put it, the old dispensation to Abraham, Moses,

and the Prophets was completed by the New. Christianity was Judaism brought to its anticipated climax.

However, except for a small group of Jewish disciples in Palestine, Syria, Greece, and Rome, the Jewish community failed to see itself completed or fulfilled. It remained stubbornly Jewish, it did not see the Christ Jesus, it saw only the man. A grave problem arose for the small struggling Christian group. Its original Jewish founders were eager to retain their Jewish roots and associations, while their new Gentile-born and Gentile-oriented leadership felt that the old connections were a hindrance to expansion. The latter carried the day. Slowly but inexorably Jews now came to be considered betrayers of a sacred trust by rejecting their opportunity of salvation. In turn, God had dissolved the old covenant. What had been meant to be glorious fulfillment ended in dismal, mutual rejection. The Jew had rejected God, and God now rejected him.

Successive portions of the New Testament and of later literature reflect this progressive separation. Jesus the Jew almost disappears, as does the Jewishness of all his disciples. The Jewishness of his tormentors and executors now becomes prominent, while pagan Pontius Pilate assumes the mantle of innocence.

At first all festivals of the new Church were closely tied to the mother religion. Easter is a good example. The New Testament placed the trial, crucifixion, and resurrection of Jesus in the Passover week, and consequently the early followers of Jesus—Jews all of them—marked the memory of these events by their customary festival calendar. When they celebrated Passover they also observed the death of Jesus at special ceremonies. In time, as more and more Gentiles joined the new sect, the memorial services for the founder assumed an independent character and eventually the connection between Passover and the new Christian festival became tenuous. But the old name lingered; it was

and still is called Passover in most European languages
(e.g., Pâques in French, Paaske in Danish) and for many
centuries the date of the Jewish Passover remained decisive
for the observance of its Christian counterpart.

In time these ties were loosened. As long as both Christianity and Judaism were persecuted by Rome, common
suffering maintained a suspicious, but forgiving bond.
When Christianity triumphed the split became complete
and the Church made sure that nothing but unconditional
surrender on the part of the Jews would right the scales.
"In order to separate Judaism altogether from their [the
Church Fathers'] Christianity," wrote Leo Baeck, a distinguished critic of Christian-Jewish relations, "there were to be
no alliances, but only absolute separation. In their opinion,
there existed a twofold God, the wicked, dark, cruel God
who was bound up with this world, the God of Judaism,
and the good, pure, spiritual, kind God who was exalted
above all and above the whole world, the God of Christianity. All redemption signifies redemption from this world
of Judaism. And for this reason the Jews themselves are the
real enemies of Christ and the true God."[6]

What had begun as a historic schism now assumed the
proportions of bitter theological warfare. Jews at first pretended to ignore the new movement; Christians could not
afford the same luxury. The Jew, with his Old Testament,
stood squarely at the portals of the new faith; he, his
covenant, and his claim to chosenness could not be overlooked. If Jesus had come to fulfill the Jewish hope and if
the world was accepting his mission, why did the Jew continue to stand outside? What was one to make of this
double conundrum: his stubborn insistence on his Old
Testament as the truth, and his physical persistence among
the nations?

Of these two riddles, the first was more easily solved.
The Old Testament, said the Church, had been true in

every way—*had been,* that is, until the Messiah had come in the person of Jesus. At that moment the Old Testament ceased to be a living law and became history. Its task was finished, the old covenant was dissolved and the new one instituted. The Torah's laws of nationhood and its ritual demands were no longer binding and meaningful. Circumcision, dietary regulations, Sabbath observance—all these, and hundreds more, had been rendered obsolete. The Law was dead.

But this could not be said of the people. They were alive and gave every indication of staying alive. They continued to practice the dead law as if it had meaning, they overlooked the obvious truths of history and chose to be blind. Their very presence in history was a subtle disclaimer of Christianity, and as the Church strove for and achieved absolute power in its realm, it felt it could not allow the disclaimer.

What to do with the stubborn remnant? They would not be converted, neither by suasion nor force. Both were tried and both failed dismally. The social structure of emerging mediaeval society suggested the answer. In Rome, Jew and Christian had together shared the role of outcast; now the Jew alone was left. What for the Christian had been martyrdom became punishment for the Jew. He was *déclassé* because of his sins, because God was reproving him for non-compliance.

Here was the Church's answer to the riddle. God purposely kept these people alive to retain them as witnesses. Here were the killers of Christ, the rejected of salvation. Their debased communal status and second-class citizenship were expressions of the divine will, and if Jews were beaten, tortured, expropriated, and exiled, this too was visited upon them because of their continued denial of the truth.

It began with Matthew's account of the trial of Jesus, which exonerates Pilate and has the Jews proclaim defi-

antly: "His blood be on us and our children."⁷ The Jews!
Even the obviously biased account of the New Testament
describes them as a mob, agitated by passion. Taking the
story at this point literally, "the Jews" were the usual
motley agglomeration of thrill seekers who have accompanied trials, scandals, executions, and public excitements
from time immemorial. They are the ones who will always
shout "Kill him"—for they want to see blood, not justice.
And this crowd, abetted by highly placed officials who
enjoyed the favor of Rome but not the confidence of their
own people, held Jewish fate past, present, and future in
their incompetent hands? So we are led to believe: the
promises of God were abrogated by the mob, and all the
untold sufferings of many generations of their descendants
were authoritatively conferred on them by this haphazard
collection of bystanders (Were there a hundred of them?
We don't even know that!). No matter, the Book said
"Guilty forever," and from here on the degradation of the
Jew had the official blessing of the Church.

And not of the Church alone. Islam was quick to follow
suit. The Moslems have replaced Israel as God's preferred
children, says the Koran. The rabbis—Mohammed calls
them Rabbanites—have tampered with the laws of Torah
because they aspired to divine honors. Abu Mohammed Ali,
a tenth-century theologian, declared the text of the Hebrew
Bible to be corrupt, "full of untruth and apocryphal, just
as Judaism is an apocryphal religion." This was an approach
somewhat different from the Christian church, but the result was the same: "Woe and alas to a religion . . . whose
untruth is thus established."⁸

According to the Koran the dietary laws of the Jews are
punishment for their heresy, and Jews are, like other
idolaters, considered enemies of Moslems while Christians
are their friends. A later Moslem tradition avers that "on

the last day the faithful will do battle with the Jews, whereupon the stones will say to the believers: 'Behind me lurks a Jew, O Moslem strike him dead.'"[9] Islam's paternoster makes the faithful pray: "Lead us in the right path, the path of those to whom Thou hast shown mercy and who have not been visited by Thy wrath and who have not strayed from Thee."[10] By traditional interpretation, the strayers are the Christians, the ones visited with divine ire are the Jews, although this ire was never unleashed on Jews in Moslem lands with the same fervor as in Christendom. Still, Paul and his teachings reached far into the Orient and commanded the Occident. The message was always the same: the Jew was spiritually degenerate and he deserved his physical debasement.

Of course there were discordant notes. There were Christian voices which doubted the accuracy of this neat solution. There were many Christians, from popes to princes, who felt uneasy with this harsh theology and tried to meliorate the daily lot of the Jews.

Forced conversion, while it was practiced occasionally, generally did not find approval from the popes, who repeated Gregory IX's prohibition against such activity, and Thomas Aquinas—who was no friend of the Jews—also rejected forcible means of overcoming Jewish obstinacy. Innocent IV took pains to point out the four reasons why Jews, despite all they had done, were to be tolerated:

Their existence was proof for the truth of the Jesus story, just as their suppressed condition was proof for the triumph of Christianity;

The Jews remained the guardians of the Old Testament even though they did not understand it properly;

Jesus himself had asked to wait patiently for the Jews' conversion; and finally,

The conversion of the Remnant had been prophesied.[11]

Still, such benevolent language could not hide the stern policy of both Church and State which restricted the freedom of Jews and which eventually limited them to ghettos, districts, and enclaves. They were used and abused, expelled and readmitted, for they remained enemies of a Christian society.

In this respect the sails of the Church were firmly set and the course charted, the will of God was known, at least as far as it concerned the fall of His former chosen ones.

The Reformation failed to reform this attitude substantially. In the beginning Martin Luther hoped that his purging of the Church would make it possible for the Jews to come to the true, purified faith. But when they refused to heed the new opportunity, the disillusioned reformer from Wittenberg turned on them with doubled fury.

In a detailed program, which his countrymen put into effect almost exactly four hundred years later, Luther specified:

One should put their synagogues and schools to the torch and should cover with dirt whatever will not burn, so that no man should ever again see a single stone or even the ashes thereof. This one ought to do for the honor of our Lord and of Christendom, that God may see that we are Christians; one should similarly wreck and destroy their homes, for there they practice what they teach in their schools. They may be herded under one roof or into a stable, like gypsies. They should be deprived of their prayer books and idolatries, lies, curses, and blasphemies. One should prohibit their rabbis, on pain of death, to teach any more. Jews should lose all privileges of using commons or streets. . . .[12]

Calvin, too, concerned himself with the Jews and like

Luther he approved of their depressed condition and suffering. In a special treatise dedicated to this subject he
came to the sad but stern conclusion that the recalcitrant
rejecters of Jesus must not be met with Christian mercy.
"Their corrupt and untamable obstinacy deserves that they
be oppressed beyond all measure through an enormous
succession of miseries and ills so that because of these
terrible experiences they will give up the ghost. And let
none show them pity!"[13]

This was written in the year 1597. The modern age was
opening windows everywhere, except for Jews dwelling in
the back streets of history. For them the shutters remained
fastened for another two hundred years.

The unbroken Christian line of solving the problem of
Jewish existence was at first knotted and then severed by
the advance of secularism. As long as men believed the
fundamental teachings of Christianity, they could absorb
and accept its attitude toward the Jews. But when the
fresh winds of emancipation blew through the eighteenth
and nineteenth centuries and shook the old sturdy faith,
the prevalent views about Jews became less believable and
finally unacceptable.

Moses Mendelssohn, Jewry's great modern philosopher,
still had to pay a cattle head tax when he entered the
gates of Berlin in 1743, and as late as 1840 English par-
liamentarians argued seriously whether Jews were really
human beings capable of citizenship. But by and large,
theologically based persecution and discrimination were re-
duced as the pillars of Christianity itself began to sway in
the earthquake of liberalism and naturalism. Jews disappeared from their position of central concern in the
Church, their riddle unsolved. Why is a Jew? Mediaeval
Christianity had pretended to know the answer; modern
Christianity no longer found it palatable and searched for
other approaches to the enigma.

THE MODERN CHRISTIAN APPROACH

Slowly but surely the religious obstinacy of the Jew began to be viewed not as God-rejection but as God-willed. Israel is needed for salvation, it will come to Christ in God's own good time, this new theology proclaimed. The Jew must therefore be loved, not hated, for he is the Christian's brother. The separateness of the Jew is a sign of his holiness, said Protestant theologian Christopher E. Luthardt a century ago: "The existence of this wonderful people shows that God has spared it for a future. If that future belongs to Jesus Christ, then Israel too belongs to Him."[14]

By and large this has remained the modern Christian approach, although it arrived too late on the scene of history to halt the poisonous spread of anti-Semitism fed from the ancient wellsprings of theology. Thoughtful Christians did not fail to recognize that the death of the six million at the hands of the Nazis was in part ascribable to Christian prejudice, to say nothing of Christian silence. No hindsight argument over Hochhuth's *Deputy* could obscure this basic fact. The guilt of Pius XII will long be debated; the contributory guilt of the old teachings from Origen to Chrysostom to Luther and Calvin is forever visible to the unbiased observer.

Not that all traces of such mediaevalism have now disappeared. Would that it were so!

As late as 1955, with the stench of Auschwitz still clinging to every German, a Protestant German catechism said that in the treatment of the Jews one cannot overlook the lesson from Matthew's Gospel: "Here, and not in the political or humanitarian realm, lies the secret of the fateful way which this people has since traversed, a way marked by blood and tears."[15]

And a valiant missionary author who has the sonorous

title of Kirchenrat says frankly that he has "always thought it childish if in looking at the persecution of Jews one sees only the wickedness of men, and especially Christians, *and not also the hand of God.*"[16]

I am the last to deny that Christians here face a serious problem—it is of course the very problem with which this book is concerned, the problem of Jewish existence. But of course my reference is not theirs, for I am not weighted down by the premise that Israel has sinned or erred in rejecting Jesus. Here the Christian must make up his mind. If he clings to the premise, then he is caught in the trap of seeming to approve the horrendous iniquities committed against the Jews by ascribing them to the nebulous realm of "God's will." Even a well-meaning contemporary theologian, once he takes the old stance, is faced with the old dilemma. I quote a Catholic writer:

God's intent, when He judges the Chosen People, is not perdition but salvation of the people. The obstinate portion of Israel (i.e., those who did not accept Jesus) was to be brought to its senses by falling from its former eminence and by experiencing all the tribulations. *Only because God cannot forget this people does He chastise it hard and often.*[17]

But there is another possibility, another road which Christians can travel to arrive at a view of Jewish existence, and this road has been increasingly used since the Hitler catastrophe. It is in fact a revolutionary departure from the past. I like to think that it heralds the new Christian view and that in time it may become dominant. I will not judge its theological justification for it is based on beliefs I do not share. I can however describe it and appreciate its effect.

This new attitude recognizes that whatever Israel ought to be has to do not only with Israel but with Christians. In judging the Jewish situation a Christian must at once judge his own and ask himself: Did I properly testify to my faith? Did I treat the Jew as my brother whom I need as much as he needs me? In the last resort, is it not the Jew who has testified more consistently than the Christian, and—from this Christian point of view—should one not say that in the long perspective of salvation the Jews died for Christ?

We must finally say it. They were taken because of Him. They were slaughtered for Him. In His place. In His stead.[18]

But this is only the beginning. It reflects the intimation of Pius XII who spoke of Jews as "adorers of Christ" even though they call Him by a different name. It prepares the next step, the revolutionary step: the acceptance of Israel as a constant factor in the divine economy, a people not to be punished or persecuted but accepted without condition, a step foreseen but not yet taken by the second Ecumenical Council. Yet already in 1947 Protestant and Catholic theologians in Germany had informally agreed on a set of theses which began by saying:

One and the same God speaks to all men through the Old and the New Testament.[19]

And the mighty voice of Karl Barth adds: "The Church must live with the synagogue, not—as the fools say in their heart—as with another religion or confession, but as with the root from which it sprang."[20] From Barth there is but a short step to Reinhold Niebuhr, who draws the ultimate conclusion: if the Jew is to be accepted as a Jew, if he is the shoot which brought forth the first flower, if he represents not an alien religion but the other side of the Christian world view, then acceptance must be total and all attempts at conversion must be forsworn. Let each covenant faith witness to its revelation and leave to God the rest.

Thus the question remains suspended, albeit in a more congenial atmosphere than in days gone by. For the new Christian it means to look after the Christian sector of the divine economy and to let the Jew look after his own. "We should not ask," says Niebuhr, "that this peculiar historical miracle fit into any kind of logic or conform to some historical analogy. It has no analogy. It must be appreciated for what it is."[21]

But what is it? Christians still ask it, so do secularists, and Jews will and must.

THE MARXISTS

Once we leave the realm of theology the field widens and there seems to be no limit to the imagination. The "peculiar treasure" which this people thought itself to be has become the treasure trove of every manner of historical interpretation.

Among these the Marxist is by far the most important, if for no other reason than that its adherents are so numerous and that it has influenced Jewish life so decisively. Karl Marx himself was born into a Jewish family. We will not trespass on the domain of the psychologists who view Marx's theory of Jewish history as a revolt against his father and as a particularly violent form of self-hatred. Briefly summarized, his teachings about Jews and Judaism—later refined and amplified by Mehring, Kautsky, and Lenin—state the following:

All religions are expressions of economic circumstances and subject to their laws. Judaism is no exception. In its various stages it reflects the nomadic, urban, mercantile and, capitalist forms of its history.

Religion is the handmaiden of the conservative, exploiting classes. Dogma, priesthood, and established cult serve their purposes. They will encourage study of the past rather than intelligent participation in the pressing problems of the day; they aim to keep the masses illiterate and ignorant, unlike secular education which promotes the desire for a fair share of life.

The masses are diverted from their plight by promises of immortality, resurrection, and other vistas of future happiness, and they are threatened with hell if they do not abide by the convenient standards of the exploiter's moral code.

Judaism no less than other religions foists the belief in a supernatural God upon the pervasive superstitions of the ignorant and suppressed masses. This God has all the power, hence men have none; this God has all the responsibility, hence men have none. If conditions are bad, if people suffer from poverty and disease, it is God's will and one must piously submit to it. Revolution is rebellion against divine order, and eternal damnation is in store for the evil ones who would advocate or—Heaven forbid!—even practice it.

Religion, then, is the opiate of the people. It keeps them content with their misery, dreaming pipe dreams of an illusory never-never land of spiritual bliss. In every clime and age this formidable alliance of exploiting clergy and upper classes has held the masses in subjugation. There is little to choose between Moslems, Christians, Buddhists, and witchcraft or voodoo. Each is a form of economic oppression. Rabbis, priests, and medicine men—they are all the same in their spheres of nefarious behavior.

Somehow, however, history has conspired to give Jews a special place. Once they were a nation, but since the beginning of the Diaspora they have occupied a unique role. They have been helpers of princes and priests by supplying them with capital and they served them—unwillingly, to be sure—as convenient scapegoats in times of popular unrest. The Jewish masses in the lands of dispersion can be liberated only if they throw off the yoke of their own religion and unite with the disinherited proletariat of the world in a common revolution against capitalism. In this struggle they are a hybrid group; they are not a class (for classes exist only in a land-possessing and capital-producing nation) but rather a caste composed of diverse elements. Their policy of liberation must be total assimilation to the universal brotherhood of men; the Jewish people may perpetuate their language and their cultural characteristics for a while, but any attempt to link the class struggle with such bourgeois concepts as Zionism must be opposed or aborted.

Judaism, that is, rabbinism in all its forms, does have purpose and meaning. Here the Marxists join hands with theologians, which is not surprising for in its realm Marxism is a quasi religion with dogmas and priests. But of course the Marxist interpretation of the Jewish God differs considerably from the God of the Jewish and Christian textbooks.

In his discussion of Judaism, Karl Marx states that its basis was and is "practical need." What is this practical need? Avarice, he says. "What is the Jews' worldly God? Money. Money is the jealous God of Israel above whom there cannot be any other God." A latter-day Soviet disciple of the Marxist doctrine hints not so darkly that the stereotype of the Jew as Mr. Moneybags is true to life and not an invention of Jew-haters. From the founder of Communism to the prosecution of Jewish doctors to the suppression of Yiddish culture and the contemporary persecution of every Jewish expression in Soviet Russia runs a straight line. When in 1964 the official propaganda bureau of the Ukraine published a book on Jews and Jewish history, with text and pictures out of Julius Streicher's late and unloved pornographic *Stürmer*, the world was surprised and communists were generally embarrassed. They should not have been. When it is official doctrine to consider the Why of Jewish existence as an expression of avarice and rabbinic economic conspiracy, why should the faithful scribbler in

Kiev not be convinced that his rehash of the founding prophet's own words would earn him encomia and advancement?[22]

This in brief is the "theology" of Marx which in respect to our problem may more properly be described as "Jewish demonology." But we cannot leave his thought without acknowledging that in one respect it also made an important positive contribution to our understanding. He took Jewish history out of its total isolation and bound it to the history of the nations and he directed our attention to the political, social, and economic conditions of the day. He paved the way for a wider grasp of historic reality. The more the pity that he was basically ignorant of Jews and Judaism and that his own personal problem made him, who commented on every important event of his time, incapable or unwilling to say a forthright word on the Russian pogroms of 1881, the rise of socialist Zionism, and the mass migrations of Jews to America. To him and to the guardians of his faith it was clear that Jews and Judaism would disappear with the disappearance of the capitalist order. The present Why of the Jew was capitalism; the question would lose its meaning in the establishment of the classless society.

SPENGLER AND TOYNBEE

Of the many historians who have dealt with the topic of Jews and Judaism two have a special interest for me. Both belong to our century and both have tried to see Israel as part of man's total journey. Both are philosophers of history and they share the belief that history has a recurrent rhythm, a discernible heartbeat. They think that, ultimately, a universal striving and meaning can be discovered behind the immense diversity of cultures and civilizations, behind man's murderous lust and his sublime achievement.

The two of whom I will speak, briefly, are Oswald

Spengler and Arnold Toynbee. Both may be described as meta-historians, that is, historians who see metaphysical, spiritual, and even mystical forces at work. Both have had and have an influential readership. What Spengler had to say was used—against his will, as he wrote later—as support for militant German hatred of the Jew; and Toynbee's critique of Jewish history has strongly reinforced certain western Christian notions among the middle-class intelligentsia who are his staunchest admirers.

Spengler was a German and a mystic. He believed he had discovered the key to the rise and fall of human civilizations, a cyclical growth-and-decay pattern which responded to spiritual rather than material impulses. He saw western civilization nearing its stage of dissolution in which it would yield to "Caesarism," the force of total dictatorship —the latter an all too accurate prophecy, as it soon turned out. Among the many elements that contribute to *The Decline of the West* (his chef d'oeuvre) the Jews play a significant role.

Spengler is not chary in his admiration of the Jew, and like most Christians he has a special warm spot for the Prophets and their "magnificent spirituality."[23] They belong to what he calls the "Arabic culture," which encompasses the entire Near East, and he coins for it the term "magic," by which he means that their religion recognizes one single absolute principle of good in contrast to other gods who are evil. "This is the foundation of the magic idea: it accepts a universal historic struggle between good and evil, in which evil gains an intermediary victory and the final triumph of good on the day of judgment. This moralization of world history is shared by Persians, Chaldeans and Jews."

Jewish existence falls into two parts: before and after the Babylonian exile. Before the Exile Jews had a history like any other people and they had a sense of history and experienced it in normal fashion with typical "racial" intensity. (I must admit that the introduction of the term "race" into the world of concepts makes it difficult to treat Spengler seriously.)

But with its displacement from the land Israel became what Spengler calls a nation by consensus. Normal nations who live on their land simply are what they are and ask few questions about their existence. They need no consensus to be. It is different with landless nations, of which Israel is [or was when Spengler wrote] the prime example. They need will and purpose to be, they are a nation not *de facto* but *e consensu*. Consequently they have no history in the real sense. Jews, says Spengler, had a history until 586 before the Christian era. The return from Babylon and the period of the Second Temple were the interim story of a minority which did not substantially or permanently alter the character of the Jewish existence. Since then Jews have been the anti-historical element in the midst of real-life, land-bound historical nations. This and not latter-day economic and sociological factors form the reason for the world's hatred of the Jew. To be sure, most men don't really understand this hatred which has to do with "the different heartbeats of two different life streams and appears as an unbearable dissonance, a hatred which can become tragic to both."

"This is the fact which has most deeply and bitterly separated Israel and the nations, a fact the full tragedy of which is least understood: while occidental man for the last 1000 years has experienced history in its most significant sense and has done so with a consciousness not equaled in any culture, the Jewish consensus has ceased to have a history. Its problems were solved, its inner forms completed and unchangeable; centuries had no more meaning for it and therefore no one who is bound to the consensus can at all comprehend the passions with which Faustian men experience their fate. ["Faustian" is Spengler's word of admiration for the essentially mystic, pagan, heroic, racially conscious, and sensuous occidental man.]

"For the Jew all this happened three millennia ago. History in the grandest manner flows by—but outside; epoch follows epoch; man changes with every century but in the ghetto and in the soul of the individual everything stands still."

The Jew is therefore international. Even when he acts like a patriot of his host nation he follows subconsciously the need of his own non-historical consensus. Therefore he supports democracy in monarchical lands and imperialism where it is possible. He is destructive of national ideals and ideas, whether he wants to or not. He only follows his fate.

What is this fate? To assist in the final destruction of the Faustian man. In America, says Spengler, this destruction has already proceeded apace, and when the American civilization joins the European in a common megalopolitan anonymity the Jew will lose his *raison d'être* and become absorbed into the mass of men. With the final decline of the West in which the Jew has from the beginning played a significant role, he finds his meaning, his fate and his fulfillment. The man-without-history helps his host culture to dissolve its history and in the process Jew and Gentile become a meaningless, decaying undifferentiated mass, only to make room for the birth of a new civilization.

Fate binds Jew and Gentile to their inner needs and drives them to the inexorable end. Spengler ends his prophecy on a note of near resignation. There is but a narrow margin for free human action although "we do not have the freedom to accomplish this or that, only the choice to do what is necessary or to do nothing at all."

Whatever meaning history may have is poured into the very lifeblood of civilizations. There it courses, determined by higher powers, until the tragedy is completed, the last

act played according to the script. With Marx it is the revolution, with Spengler "Caesarism" that opens the penulti-
mate scene; with both, man is little more than an actor
declaiming before an unseen, uncaring audience. Theirs are
views I can describe but not accept. Neither the pseudo-
scientific demonology of the one nor the mystic skepticism
of the other fill my heart and mind with a responsive Yes.

Marx and Spengler are determinists, and Arnold Toynbee is at first blush not different. He too sees a rise, growth,
and decay of societies. His assessment and assignment of
civilizations is his own as is his basic recurrent theme of challenges and responses. But where Marx and Spengler were
non-Christian in motivation and approach, Toynbee is a
Christian through and through. His faith colors his historic
view and it is no wonder that when he comes to the Jews
he sees them with the old, darkened spectacles of his religion. That is a pity, for Toynbee has many readers, even
if his fellow historians think little of the persistent accuracy
of his information.

It is not my purpose to debate Jewish history with the
English historian. This has been done in great detail by
others, and most successfully by Maurice Samuel, whose
book *The Professor and the Fossil* is written with that rare
triple combination of erudition, magnificent prose, and subtle wit.[24] My purpose is more modest: a brief consideration
of Toynbee's view of the Jewish Why in the past and present.

Spengler considers the Jews a part of *Arabic* culture.
Toynbee calls his division *Syriac* civilization. Like Spengler,
he approves of the prophetic period and like him considers
this to be the apex of Jewish history. What comes thereafter is anticlimax. But one more important event happened
in Jewish history: the arrival of Jesus. Here was the one
opportunity to make the universal message of the Prophets
into the religion of mankind; here was a chance to break

lam, even though this was then still six hundred years in the future. Apparently Toynbee considers Islam to have been another, though not so manifest destiny of the Jews, another opportunity flung away.

But at least the renowned historian makes his point clear. The Why of Jewish existence was to be answered by the creation of a universal world religion. This was the Jewish *raison d'être* from the beginning. A descent from the universal into the national is a betrayal of destiny, a petrifaction of the spiritual impulse. This is not true for all peoples but it is true for Jews. They have a special responsibility to man and they are especially accountable to history because they invented the concept of the Chosen People, a concept which Toynbee holds is the reason why Christianity and Islam exhausted themselves in internecine warfare.

"Chosen People" is the most destructive idea ever perpetrated on man, according to Toynbee. It is the disease of extreme ethnocentrism which Christians and Moslems inherited from the Jews. It leads to claims of exclusive truth, of exclusive salvation; it leads to inquisition and auto-da-fé, to hatred, arrogance, racial strife, and all other ancillary afflictions.

If the Jew has any task left at all, it is to renounce chosenness and particularism and to lead the world toward universal values. For Toynbee, the concept of Zionism and the reality of Israel are dreadful regressions because they fortify Jewish narrowness and prevent revivification of the fossilized people. As a true Christian mystic, he is deeply angered by this most recent Jewish waywardness, angered to a degree totally unbecoming the Olympian historian.

Of this reality and the value of the Chosen People concept I will speak in a later chapter; nor will I enter here into a discussion of Toynbee's assessment of Jewish universalism and Jewish nationalism. This is a legitimate, even im-

the narrow confines of Palestinian Pharisaism and bur
through to a world-embracing mission. Alas, the Jew
missed their one chance, and consequently their history wa.
over. Thereafter they were a historic fossil—a somewhat in-
elegant version of Spengler's "people without a history." In
later writings Toynbee modified his assessment of the Jews
as fossils, but his essential approach never changed:

In deliberately refusing the opportunity that was offered it of
realizing its manifest destiny of flowering into Christianity by
opening its heart to the gospel of its Galilean step-child, Judaism
not only stultified its spiritual past but forfeited its material future
into the bargain. In declining to recognize its expected Messiah
in Jesus, Judaism was renouncing its birthright in two great enterprises which eventually made the respective fortunes of two
different daughters of Judaism by whom these enterprises were
duly carried out in the fulness of time. In the first place, Judaism
was abandoning the fallow and fertile mission-field of the Hellenic universal state to a Christian Church that was to be driven
into independence by its eviction from the Jewish fold; and in
the second place Judaism was leaving to an Islam whose founder
was to be rebuffed by the Jewish Diaspora in his native Hijaz
the subsequent political task of reuniting a Syriac World which
had been divided against itself as one consequence of the forcible intrusion of Hellenism upon Syriac ground. Instead of embracing either of these alternative opportunities for a great career when it had the refusal of both of them, Judaism preferred
to fling itself into the forlorn hope of Zealotism—in order to be
retrieved as a mere fossil.[25]

The matter is really simple once one has the proper Toynbee perspective. Jews had a "manifest destiny," which was
Christianity. (This is orthodox Christian teaching and has
little to do with historic assessment.) This fatal Jewish error was compounded because, as later events would show,
it led to another disaster. By rejecting Jesus, Jews also became responsible for the rejection, birth, and growth of Is-

portant debate, in which Jews themselves hold totally different points of view. But I cannot leave the subject without recording one personal observation.

One might forgive Toynbee many things, among them his arbitrary judgment of the revival of Hebrew as a spoken language. The erudite professor is not expected to know Hebrew, although it is a pity that he doesn't. Else he would hardly have called the return of the Jews to the language of the Torah, Prophets, and Psalmists "the laborious and ludicrous expedient of fabricating the 'mother-tongue' that they are determined to possess, in the temper of a nouveau-riche who furnishes himself with portraits of appropriate ancestors."

But what is one to think of a historian who in full view of the facts compares the Nazi extermination of the Jews to Jewish treatment of Arabs in the war of 1948 and, after this gratuitous "comparison," manages to say that actually the Jews were more guilty than the Nazis?

"The Jews had had much more experience than the Germans had had of the sufferings they were inflicting. If the Nazis were debarred from filing the plea that they knew not what they did, the Jews were debarred *a fortiori.*"

Such confusion of facts and values is extraordinary in so literate a man and unfortunately renders much of everything else of his writings thoroughly suspect. One can comprehend this lapse only as an outflow of Toynbee's ambivalent mystical relation to the Jewish people: he admires it for its magnificent potential and despises it for its failure to live up to it. To him, Jewish existence has meaning indeed, and since this meaning is bound up with the nerve centers of humanity, the Jew's fate is of crucial importance to man. Where will it turn: unto itself and the stultified past already studded with rejection and failure, or unto the universal society which awaits the Jew, as it were, as the harbinger of the Messianic age?

There is one other secular interpreter of Jewish history whose theory I must touch upon. Late in his life, when he was a refugee from the Nazis, Sigmund Freud completed his study of the origins of Judaism. The details of his theory have not attracted a significant following even among his devoted disciples, and historians as well as archaeologists have conclusively shown that his facts were not in order or were so selectively used by him as to render them useless in serious historiography.

But Freud, with all his shortcomings and errors, is not so easily disposed of, and his assessment of the destiny of Israel is singular enough to merit consideration. For he particularizes the general approach to Judaism of classical psychoanalysis which has been amplified by his followers.

Briefly, his theory, which he expounded in his *Moses and Monotheism,* states:[26]

Moses was an Egyptian nurtured on the monotheistic religion of the imaginative Pharaoh Akhnaton. It was Moses' drive and leadership which pulled his illiterate, obstreperous, and unwilling Hebrew followers from the relative comforts of their existence and led them to an uncertain future in the desert, toward a land which he told them their God had promised them. Moses was successful at first but from time to time his wards slipped back into idolatrous practices and staged violent rebellions. In one of these uprisings Moses was killed by the people who set up a false Moses in his stead and who thereafter were weighed down with the guilt of murdering the great founder-father, the very Son of God.

A thousand years later a Galilean named Jesus let himself be killed in order to expiate the ancient guilt. His followers believed themselves released from sin by identifying themselves with Jesus' sacrifice. The followers of Jesus were Jews who could now say: "It is true that we killed the primeval god (Moses) but we Christian Jews have finally admitted it and through Jesus have atoned for it. But you other Jews will not face your guilt, you reject the atonement offered you and therefore, forever after, you will have to keep on feeling guilty."

This guilt was the recurring theme of the Prophets, and the trials and tribulations of the Jewish people in the centuries to follow were obvious retributions for the primeval sin. Jews felt that they deserved nothing better than to be punished by God. "The need for satisfying this feeling of guilt which—coming from a much deeper source—was unsatiable, made them render their religious precepts ever and ever more strict, more exacting, but also more petty. In a new transport of moral asceticism the Jews imposed on themselves constantly increasing moral instinctual renunciation and thereby reached—at least in doctrine and precept—ethical heights that had remained inaccessible to the other peoples of antiquity."

And just as the Jews are subconsciously struggling to right the old wrong—and at the same time both love and hate the "Moses religion"—their Christian contemporaries, beset by similar ambivalencies toward their own religion (which is nothing but a paganized Judaism), can work out their guilt and hatred by hating the unredeemed Jew. The latter struggles on through history, his fate formed by the towering figure of Moses, his ethic shaped to meet his need for renunciation and expiation, his future darkened wherever Christians stand across his path, loading their guilt on him. All this makes the Jews what they are. But, says Freud—and it is a big but—"how they could survive until today as an entity has not proved so easy to solve. One cannot, however, reasonably demand or expect exhaustive answers of such enigmas."

Having said that much, Freud would say no more. He had moved outside the Jewish community (although briefly forced back by Hitler), and perhaps no longer felt the urge to pursue the enigma. Was it his hope that other Jews might do as he had done: recognize their tribal guilt and, by facing it, transcend all further need for the religion of Moses? Perhaps. But if Freud was no longer troubled by the clerical riddle, many still are, and they still ask the question. Freud's insights seem too remote for them; too speculative, too little founded on discernible will, and too little heedful of a religion which is neither illusion nor neurosis.

Of the Freudians and post-Freudians none has studied the implications of Jewish history and Jewish symbolism more closely than Theodor Reik. Far more versed in Near Eastern and biblical scholarship than his master he offers his insights as a "discovery in archaeological psychoanalysis." "I remain loyal to Freud," he writes, "in the conviction that psychoanalytic research into neglected corners of historic tradition is the royal road to the uncovering of forgotten meanings and tangled emotions in the life of culture."[27] He agrees with Freud in ascribing to Moses a position of supreme importance in the formation of the people and its cultic practices, but he departs from him in denying that Moses and the religion he represented were Egyptian in origin.

Reik's inquiry is concerned with the events at Sinai, which he considers the key to the understanding of Israel's origins. The revelation was an initiation rite, but one radically different from other contemporaneous ceremonies. It no longer dealt with a special class of people—young men, virgins, priests—but with the whole people. In this way it was at once more "primitive" (this being the most ancient form of initiation) and more "advanced" (because it was at once timeless and ageless). Here lay the roots of monotheism, democracy and a people's priestly vocation; here lay the foundations of Israel's special spiritual direction.

But how this came to pass and why, Reik does not profess to know, even though he is writing, by his own admission, "conjectural history." He would agree with a modern scholar who declared that when all is said and done, "the origin of Israel and its faith is left quite without adequate explanation."[28]

Why is a Jew? Freud did not answer the query and neither did his epigones. It still stands out boldly against the mind's horizon. And so we return to the beginning. If the non-theologians do not hold the answer or are satisfied to let the question rest as insoluble; if the Jewish theologians of the past can no longer speak to many of us and the Christian theologians are hemmed in by yesterday's guilt and today's doubts, where shall we turn? Why should a Jew persist in being a Jew—or should he?

IN FINE: JEWISH HUMANISTS

Of course, there is one other possible way of treating this question and that is to declare it basically irrelevant and meaningless. This has in fact been done by some of the most renowned Jewish analysts of the last hundred years.[29] Although in many ways they tend to overlap, they fall into three broad groups.

One group may be described as nationalist and is represented by such figures as Moses Hess, Perez Smolenskin, Ahad Ha-Am, Simon Dubnow, and the political Zionists. These men looked at world history and saw that nationalism was the crest of a new wave of civilization. Nations defined the content of politics and the shape of culture, and nations did not need to justify themselves. Men are endowed with certain inalienable rights, the Jeffersonians had declared, and the conviction that each national group had the right of self-determination became a hallowed international principle. Woodrow Wilson merely enunciated it memorably; its truth was not new, but was considered self-evident, as if part of some pervasive natural law. (With well over one hundred nations now forming the United Nations, mankind seems today to have given formal assent to nationalism as man's normal and expected basis for organization. That at the moment of its greatest success this world outlook would have to give way to larger concepts which would of necessity once more limit all national self-expressions could not have been foreseen two generations ago.)

When nationalism was rising to its full eminence, and Jewish nationalists, especially in Eastern Europe, demanded recognition for "national Jewish aspirations," they did not find it relevant to ask why Jews needed or ought to survive; they were what they were and that sufficed. Jews had ethical and cultural values all their own; they cherished them and were entitled to sustain and develop them. They spoke Yiddish, many loved and knew Hebrew as a literary tongue, and language too came into the vortex of cultural treasures. Some looked for autonomous national life within some East European state, others searched for a fresh territory in Australia or Africa, but the majority looked to Palestine where Jews would establish a new society in the old land. Political and cultural Zionism were the godchildren of nineteenth-century nationalism, and present-day Israel still exhibits, as we shall see later on, strong traces of the old philosophy which eschews all need to ask for a Why of Jewish existence.

The second group are the socialists. At first they drew their inspiration from the classical writings of Marx and his successors, which meant that nationalism like religion was decried as a tool of exploitation. Consequently, national Jewish survival was of no particular concern to them. They opposed the study of Hebrew as a device to bring antiquated or reactionary ideas back into Jewish life. Their final goal was the salvation of man, a goal for which all past values had to be sacrificed.

But some of the socialists combined their political philosophy with a fervent Jewish nationalism, long before Stalin raised the concept of "revolution in one land" to international communist respectability. Through their writings and their labor they laid the foundations of a Jewish labor movement and of co-operative enterprises upon which much of present-day Israel is built. They revived the latent element of Jewish Messianism in secular garb: Jewish ethics and social vision could reclaim the desert, reclaim the ghetto-warped, urban Jew, and at the same time set a magnificent example to the world. It was a bold commitment to the future and it was undertaken without recourse to esoteric questions of meaning.

All of these men are humanists, that is, they derive their values from human existence and not from any supernatural source. But some of them hold religious convictions in the broad sense and therefore are described, rather awkwardly, as religious humanists. They form the third group and are found primarily in the Diaspora. Their most vocal advocate today is our own contemporary Mordecai M. Kaplan.

The personal, caring God of the Jewish past recedes into a vague, general, universal "force," which "makes for salvation." In the sight of such a force there can be no choosing and no chosen ones. But Jews can and must continue to choose the ethics of their tradition voluntarily, as a religious avocation, and this will set them aside as well as assure their survival. If Jews will practice Judaism, with its splendid, proven ways and ideals, they will guarantee their own existence. It is a survivalist philosophy, centered on Israel as the core, a "Judaism without supernaturalism."[30]

Its adherents share a burning conviction that their people survived in the past and will survive in the future only because of a national "will to survive." They are Jews, deeply committed to Jewish values, and hence it seems needless to ask "Why?" We are Jews and within us courses a collective *élan vital*. It is our task to release it, to bring its beneficent potential to flower in the life of Jew and Gentile. It may be hard to be a Jew, but it is also good to be one. How poor I would be if I, born into this glorious heritage, would let it wither or would eschew it altogether; how poor the world would have been without my people, how poor it would be without it in the years to come! Live, and do not ask, "Why live?" Our premise is not God or psychology, our premise is the living Jew, scion of a noble people, who is now and always called upon to take up the greatest vocation on earth: to be himself at his best. He is not chosen, nor is he superior, but he can choose to become, if not always superior to them, then at least equal in excellence to the nations of the world and thereby fulfill himself and make his singular contribution to mankind. This contribution is one which no one else can make, for only the Jew can give to human life that special modality which has distinguished him from the beginning.

It is an attractive way of looking at myself. I must admit it. I like to look into the mirror and see the man of potential and, seeing him, say to myself: I am indeed part of a great and worth-while enterprise. Accepting oneself is psychologically necessary.

But what if the mirror is clouded or my lids are heavy with restless doubt? What if in the dusk of day the doubts have not been dispelled and the question remains? Can one hold that Jewish values are so unique, so decidedly different from the best in other cultures that they must be preserved at any price? That Jewish poetry or fiction is singular beyond duplication? That Jewish family life is *sui generis*? That Jewish ethics are a phenomenon of rare distinction? That, all in all, this people needs perpetuation for its own sake and the sake of the world—*at any price*?[31]

True—Jewish values are unique. Their peculiar grace is hard to detect in isolated instances; it is felt rather than seen. It is a mixture of law and leniency, of resignation to a God with whom one is almost unduly familiar, an unyielding righteousness tempered by humorous acknowledgment of human foibles, an unreasonable optimism tinged by a large grain of skepticism and a pinch of cynicism, a view of the Jewish self which is both adulatory and deprecatory, it is—to put it in American terms—a bit of Brooklyn, a bit of Grant's Iowa rectitude, and a section of the public library, all distilled and bound into a folio of Talmudic discussion. Everything is reminiscent of something else, but the whole has a quality all its own. (But, you will say, has not every people its distinctiveness? What is there in Jewish uniqueness to make it worth ignominy and martyrdom?)

True—Jewish writing is unlike the writing of other cultures. There is nothing quite like the poetry of Bialik or the stories of Sholom Aleichem. There is in fact nothing like Yiddish for expressing the spirit of Diaspora. (There is of course also nothing like Milton or Pushkin, and like English, Russian, or any literary tongue.)

True—there was something special about the Jewish family and about Jewish ethics. I say "was," because in the maelstrom of modern life these singularities have been colored so heavily by their environment that few distinctive qualities remain. Even in divorces, alcoholism, and delinquency Jews are making large steps backward. All these bellwethers of social and psychological disturbance were rare among Jews in past generations. They are no longer so. At best we can say that Jewish tradition still harbors the potential for outstanding ethical performance. (But is it alone in that?)

It is not the purpose of this book to describe these singularities in detail. Their catalogue belongs under the caption "What is a Jew?", a roster drawn up by many highly vocal and competent interpreters. But in the end one question remains: Are all these distinctions and attributes of the Jewish people the essential *raison* for survival, or are they merely a by-product of Jewish existence? In the end the humanists would hold the former; I hold the latter.

It is true that every collective has survival qualities of one sort or another; at its lowest level it relies on the law of sheer inertia. The higher the ratio of true or imagined other characteristics, the higher the likelihood of survival. This is true for a club, an institution, or a nation. But a "will to survive" is a biological and perhaps psychological reality; it is not a motive force in a collective, and certainly cannot be demonstrated to have existed per se among Jews as an identifiable will of its own. And neither can we speak of Jews wishing to perpetuate Jewish values for their own sake.

No, Jews did not survive as a people because they had better human, hygienic, and social attributes and habits. They did not survive because they were a more stubborn breed than others. They did not survive because their sociological structure favored continued existence. They survived because they believed—no less, no more.

They believed in their covenant with God, they believed in His faithfulness, they often believed in their own superiority and in their exclusive religious prerogatives. *They did not develop their faith as a support for survival; in the past it was always the other way around; Jewish existence made sense and was possible only because the Jew believed in his divinely determined status.*

But the past is gone and Jewish faith has shifted its ground, if it has not weakened to the point of disappearance. Men like Kaplan are certainly right in making these changes their great concern. But they cannot be right in their proposal to make faith a handmaiden of survival, its "gelatinous preserve," as Arthur A. Cohen called it, a handy tool to achieve what Jews desire. For why should we Jews survive at all?

I will put it baldly: *There seems to be no reason at all why we should,* no reason, that is, which can be expressed culturally, politically, psychologically, sociologically. We may have been unique, but uniqueness is no value in itself. To survive for survival's sake may be enough for others; it is not enough for Jews. Other peoples do not spend time arguing their need for being. They are; that is sufficient unto itself. It is apparently—but only apparently!—sufficient even for Israelis in Israel. The Jew as a supranational being, however, asks the question.

Do not say: Why ask? Enough that he does, for apparently he must. Why is a Jew—and why ought he persist in being a Jew tomorrow?

Out of loyalty to his forebears? Loyalty has its limits. They had their needs, we have ours. They cannot obligate us forever.

Because we are superior, better in some undefinable way? We are not.

Because we could be examples to mankind in social behavior and ethical pursuits? I doubt it. Little in our present conditions of assimilation gives credence to such a likelihood.

Because of our folkways? Hardly.

Because of anti-Semitism? No one will seriously suggest that prejudice should be a *raison d'être* for Jews. It may be a factor for cohesion (unless it is a factor for destruction), but the means can never be the end.

What then? With church and humanist, historian, social analyst, and psychologist struggling to find a rationale for Jewish existence today, where shall we turn in the even more complex search for the Why of a Jewish tomorrow? With the old faith gone, the sure ground of saying the unqualified Yes has disappeared.

CHAPTER III

The Long Moment

Why did the Holy One, blessed be He,
choose Israel? Because . . . Israel
chose the Holy One, blessed be He, and
His Torah.

Midrash
Numbers Rabba

Where do we turn from here? Back to the beginning, to a
more detailed examination of each unlikely incident of Israel's impossible history? Try it, and you will find that
every door through which you pass in your search for
greater knowledge will lead you to other portals hiding further improbabilities. It is a vast and strange edifice, this
house of Jewish history, filled with labyrinthian paths and
mysterious scented curtains which, when drawn aside, reveal questions rather than answers.

To be sure, each of these questions can perhaps in some
fashion yield to some form of explanation. There is challenge and response here, reaction to pressure there, sociological inertia at one time and superstitious imitation at
another. Taken separately, piece by piece, impossibilities
dissolve into improbabilities and become coincidences for
which probability factors can be adduced. Other nations too
have such strange and unlikely chapters in their histories.
What accounts for the shifting winds which ruined the

Persian fleet at Salamis and the Spanish Armada in the English Channel? Is the picture of Henry IV, proud German emperor, kneeling in the freshly fallen snow at Canossa, a predictable event? Is the failure of Hitler to pursue the English at Dunkirk really different from the failure of Sennacherib to complete his capture of Jerusalem? One by one each people comes forward and presents its catalogue of historic mutations: the concentration of musical genius in nineteenth-century Germany, the abundance of artistic glory in Michelangelo's Italy and Rembrandt's Netherlands, the remarkable confluence of the Madisons, Jeffersons, Paines, and their contemporaries in America—are they truly different in kind from the rise of literary prophecy in ancient Israel? Is the spread of Christianity and Islam less a marvel than the encapsuled survival of a small and stubborn people?

THE NARROW, SWAYING BRIDGE OF FAITH

Or perhaps one makes a fundamental error in the question itself. Perhaps there is no such thing as "Jewish history," but only Jewish histories, perhaps the search for total meaning is but a quixotical chase? It is possible, for there is no limit to human ingenuity, and historians must by definition display both erudition and ingenuity.

One can make out a superficial case for saying that a Moroccan Jew in his destitute *mellah* has but a tenuous link with the history of twentieth-century Jewry in suburban America. For on the surface there seems indeed but little which connects one with the other. The average Jew in Casablanca has little to commend him to the Jew in Iowa, Calgary, or Washington; his folkways, his traditions, his education, even his religious practices seem utterly strange— and vice versa. The North African has his cultural roots intertwined with the descendants of Omar; the North American Jew speaks with some sentiment of John Alden and Roger Williams. One looks to the tradition of Sultans, the other to the decisions of Supreme Courts. They know little of each others' inner story; they have prejudicial notions of the others' wealth or poverty, education or lack thereof, their irreligiosity or piety as the case may be. There is a deep chasm that divides the two. They seem at first glance to belong to a Jewish polyhistory but not to one purposive "monohistory." The parts do not make a whole.

Or do they? The trouble with all these facts is that they are correct separately but not necessarily conclusive enough to justify the denial of Jewish history. For there is one matter we cannot overlook: the Jew in Marrakesh and the Jew in Manhattan *think* they belong together—despite all their mutual ignorance of each other and despite all their divergencies. Across the chasm runs a narrow, swaying bridge of faith. Across it walk the hopes and prayers of one single people who say "Yet are we one" in the face of all the fragmentary analyses.

For that is what they are: fragmentary approaches to our single question. There is *Gestalt* to Jewish existence, and its totality is more than its component parts. It is like a stream wending its way through time and space—a stream composed of molecules in unending combinations, water and minerals, plants and fish. There are the river banks and the trees shading it, the bridges which span it and the rapids down which it cascades. All this is "the river." It has a personality and a name.

So it is with history. Its flow contains the many segments of social, political, and economic reality, and they in turn relate to geographic and psychological circumstances. For example, the story of Canada is the story of the English and the French and the tension between them; but it is also the story of the Eskimos and the Ukrainians, of Labrador ice and Saskatchewan prairie, of Hudson Bay and Victoria

Island. Isolate each from the other and you have valid accounts as far as they go; still, none will tell you of national feelings and national history.

The Jew is no different. Concentrate exclusively on the parts and the whole disappears from view. But look at Jewish history from the watchtower of time and you will see it all, in its manifold parts, its colorful variants, its contributory streams. Jews thought and think of themselves as one people, and who is to tell them that their sense of peoplehood was or is illusory? Such sophistry reminds one of the grammarian who insists that the living language conform to "his" rules—that is, to ivory tower analyses composed from the vital entrails of speech. Yet the people will speak, and Jews will continue to live Jewish history, conscious of one fate, one purpose, one goal. Here *credo, ergo sum*—I believe, therefore I am—becomes reality, and the will, substance. Jewish history is, at least in part, an article of faith.

And its meaning? In the last resort it can be no less. Study each phase of Israel's existence separately, isolate all factors sufficiently, interrelate them properly with other historiographic data, and you may arrive at a comprehensible segment of human history. Circumstances may appear unusual, the odds against their occurrence great, but the unusual and extraordinary are not absent in the story of man.

Is Israel different? Each of its historic improbabilities will with some effort yield to reasonable explanations. The occurrence of prophecy and the creation of literary wealth may be ascribed precisely to that which makes them appear unlikely. For instance, we said earlier that the land of Israel, that narrow pathway of armies linking Egypt and Mesopotamia, was an improbable place for the emergence of unique ideas. Yet it may also be described as the breeding ground for fertile ideas which were here brought to hybridization; the human stock of Israel may be considered as selected in the Darwinian sense, the fittest survivors of repeated devastations. To describe the birth of great spiritual power in this locus is to say no more than that the rise of Greek culture was a truly remarkable, unlikely incident in world history, or that no historian of the eighth century could have foreseen the development of world law from the descendants of the wolf-suckled twins in swampy Latium. Assiduous scholarship has uncovered why all this should and could have occurred, and on the whole the student of world history seems satisfied that it was so. Besides, it is the improbable that is the spice of the tale.

But what are we to say of coincidences repeated beyond the breaking point of credulity? What are we to say of the unlikely added once too often to the improbable? Take each isolated "impossibility" in Jewish history and it will dissolve into believable reality, if for no other reason than that it happened and thus was possible after all. But add event to event, add survival to death and faith to disbelief, the probable to the improbable, the separated to the whole, and there emerges a story of three thousand years which is either an odd petrified remnant of the past, a fossilized imitation of life, or a weird illusion shot through with meaningless martyrdom—or it is yet something else.

I believe that it is something else. I admit that logic, history, and psychology can only point the way but offer no proof. Meaning and purpose are beyond proof. They are assumptions. We call them theories in science, acts of faith in the human realm of will and deed. I see Jewish history as such an auto-da-fé, which burns to illumine, not to destroy or be destroyed. It burns like the biblical bush, beyond the reach of physical laws.

THE SINGLE THEME

Jewish history in all its manifestations, reflects one single theme, or better, one conviction: that Israel was God's chosen. Already from the days of Abraham was Jewish history limned. His descendants were to be as numerous as the sand by the sea, and they would be a blessing to all mankind. Through ages of hope and despair, agony and victory, this ancient promise was seen in evidence and the historians of the people faithfully recorded its slow but inevitable fulfillment. If Israel is faithful, God's plan can be put into effect; if Israel becomes truly "a kingdom of priests and a holy nation," the world at large will see salvation.

In this conviction everything that happens to man—and to Israel especially—stands in direct relation to the great promise, a promise repeated to the Patriarchs, confirmed at Sinai and attested to by the generations thereafter. Jewish history is world history condensed to its quintessence; it is the hub of events; if all is well with Israel, the world is well; if Israel is ailing, mankind is ill.

In a direct way then human history is the responsibility of the Jew, for it is ultimately he to whom the fate of man is entrusted. God and man wait on the perfection of the Jew.

It is a grand, if "unreasonable" conception. But then, is grandeur ever reasonable? It is self-centered, no doubt about that. It glorifies Jewish choice, Jewish potential, Jewish hope. It magnifies Jewish failings into proportions of world catastrophe. But make no mistake about it: grandeur is always and forever a position of utter responsibility. It may appear ludicrous to hear a numerically insignificant section of mankind proclaim itself the guardian of human fate, but at the same time this strange people is willing to assume all the burdens that such a task implies. If it is to be ignominy, let it be so. If it is to be dispersion, it must be endured. If it is to be martyrdom, this must be borne. The promise of reward is vague and distant. Meanwhile a loving God, like a good father, chastises His beloved children with punishments of love. He is harsher on them because they aspire so high, because divinely and humanly, *noblesse oblige*.

All of this is an unreasonable basis for national history. It is an unreasonable reason for national survival. But there has been no other. Without it Jewish history would be unimaginable. The Jewish Why has always related to God. Sectional histories may tell fascinating tales and appear unique in color and texture, but they all belong to the same priestly kingdom, the same hope, the same expectation: they all fit under the wings of the Shekina. Jewish history posits a caring, choosing God—and without this knowledge one can know nothing of Israel's history.

And here precisely lies the reason for the failure of all purely secular approaches to the fate of this people. They deal with what Arthur A. Cohen calls the "natural Jew" —but the natural Jew's natural history will only be one part of the whole. It is the "supernatural Jew," the Jew in relation to a suprahistorical *raison d'être,* whose presence must be accounted for. He is the vital part of the eternally vital people. His eye is fixed on matters beyond economics and politics, he speaks of purpose and goals, and he always speaks of God.

A people so oriented cannot live on that ordinary plain of existence where mere being is sufficient unto itself. The raw struggle for the barest livelihood may have filled the worrying days and nightmarish hours of mankind for many of history's dragging centuries; for the Jew it was a means to an end, not an end in itself. The hope for the Messiah's arrival never quite left this people's soul and until that day Israel would witness to the God of its fathers.

This was not just priestly or rabbinic theology, it was the life-giving daily sustenance of the high and the low, the educated and the *am haaretz,* whose literacy was circumscribed by prayer book and psalms. The prayer book especially was the active ingredient in this approach to Jewish meaning. From one end of the earth to the other Jews were molded by its aspirations, petitions, hopes. "Thou hast chosen us" was a conviction oft repeated with these or similar words. "We are Thy people, Thou art our God"—this was the daily theme of the liturgy. The *Siddur*, the regular prayer book, was the Jew's repository of popular theology. The merchant in Verona, the wagon driver in Dublin, and the hod carrier in Salonica, all acquired from it the knowledge that they were carrying the Torah for the Holy One, that they were His representatives among the children of men. If there came a time to witness for Him—and it came often enough—witness they did, with life and limb, for *kiddush ha-shem* as it came to be called, for the sanctification of His name.

For it was not enough to be the people of His choice, loved and chastised as no one else. It is not enough to be an object, not even of love. One has to be an active partner, in human as well as in divine enterprises. If Israel needed God to mark its destiny, then God needed Israel in turn to accomplish His plans.

God needing man! A bold yet comforting concept. Israel, the people needed by God—it was a conviction which filled the last capillaries of the humblest existence. It gave life, direction, and verve to the hunted, for at the end of the road waited God with strong hand and outstretched arm, saying: "I have waited for you!"

So they told stories and wove legends about the waiting God and the waiting Messenger. They told of Elijah the prophet, returned to earth, sitting among the beggars in the gates of Rome. Accosted by a simple Jew, Elijah reveals that the Messiah, whose harbinger he was known to be, was ready to come and redeem the world. "But why does He wait?" asks the Jew asking for all his people. "For whom does He wait?" And Elijah: "He waits for you, only for you . . ."

God waits for me—what a frightening and yet magnificent thought! If I believe this, then the darkest night reveals the glimmer of a rising sun, then I can see hope where no one else can, then against the might of impossible odds I will bear the stiff neck of unshakable optimism. I will cry with Job: "Though He slay me, yet will I believe."[1]

This "yet" of unreasonable faith in the face of crudely obstructing circumstance has received a special flavor in its Hebrew formulation. *Af al pee khen* is the idiom expressing the "and yet" of Jewish optimism. Literally it means just that: "Despite what (reality) seems to say, I say Yes."

And with this conviction handed from father to son for endless generations the smallest detail of daily life was devoted to the service of the Most High. Custom was hallowed to His name, tradition became law and the law was commanded of God and hence called *mitzvah*. Literally the word means "commandment," "that which God asks us to do." But because *mitzvah* was also the gateway to the people's future it was filled with anticipation and pleasure. *Mitzvah* then was both commandment and joy, from the greatest *mitzvah* to the smallest. And the rabbis were wont to stress that no man could know which *mitzvah* was great and which was small, for that which appears negligible in human eyes may be essential in the eyes of God.

So were the days filled with prayer and with deeds of service to God and man, with the candle of saving hope shining in the long corridor of human time. God was at the center of Jewish history, and however strong the centrifugal thrust of dispersion, God was the centripetal power which kept this people within the periphery of meaningful existence.

I say "God was at the center" as if it was a historical fact that He was. God's centrality in history was to the Jew no mere subjective assumption, no self-serving supposition which explained the otherwise inexplicable. Either He is and is the God of the Covenant, or He is fiction and the Covenant a retrospective illusion. In the former case history makes sense and no *mitzvah,* no sacrifice is too demanding. But if the latter be true, if the God of Sinai is the desperate invention of a desperate people, then not only is this people's existence the cruelest joke perpetrated on poor, misled, ignorant men, but the most improbable factor is added to the star-studded roster of Jewish historical improbabilities. If God is not, then the impossibilities of Jewish history are made possible only by the maintenance of a fiction, a final grandiose Zero giving meaning and structure to all the rest.

But it cannot be so, and I believe it is not so. I believe in a God of history, I believe in a Covenant, albeit the venture of my faith may differ in many ways from that of my fathers. I believe in it not because history demands such faith, although I hold that history strongly supports it. The roots of one's belief are hard to isolate. They have to do with childhood prayers and adolescent rebellion, with the touch of awe and the tears of sorrow, with the struggle for meaning and the sudden fleeting glimpse of Truth, with nagging doubt and triumphant "and yet."

So at least it has been with me, and the last chapter of this book will deal with these personal approaches to my faith. The older I become the more the force of the Covenant speaks to me, and the more do I want to speak of it to all who will listen. *The riddle of the Jew is at heart the riddle of Sinai.* In this respect I stand with my fathers and their answer. But while they thought that they knew much that was to be known about it—for Torah and tradition had told them much—modern man must face it from the beginning. Said Moses: "I make this covenant, with its sanctions, not with you alone, but both with those who are standing here with us this day before the Lord our God and with those who are not with us here this day."[2] Tradition adds that every generation of Jews should consider itself to have stood at Sinai and to have answered: "We will do and we will hearken."

What one will do with this, forms the content of one's existence. One can disregard it, and Jewish life becomes a chimera haunting the wings of history with monstrous laughter. Or one confronts it, starting with plausibility and progressing to probability and finally to reality. And when this reality is truly faced, then suddenly we stand at Sinai and the thunder bursts relentlessly about our deafened ears. Then there is for us too the voice and the question and the silence. And there is One waiting for the answer.

THE B'RITH

The Hebrew word for covenant is *b'rith*. Wherever it is used in the Bible it connotes a fact, a confrontation of two partners. It is founded on trust; it makes the goal of *b'rith* the common possession of the covenanters. Once it is concluded, the two parties have a mutual concern that the other might be both willing and able to meet his share of the agreement. The fate of the one becomes the fate of the other. The *b'rith* alters the relationships of those who conclude it; it expands and restricts them. Possibilities are created and others denied; what could not be done alone can be achieved together, and at the same time the freedom of each partner is diminished by the presence of the other, for the *b'rith* is obligation and obligation makes incalculable demands. It exists until it is dissolved by mutual consent. Dereliction of the one does not force its dissolution but constitutes a declaration of intent. The other one may or may not act upon it. Such is the *b'rith*. Once launched upon the sea of events it has a life of its own; it sails like a ship with two masters but one tiller. They guide the vessel and it in turn carries them. Once they are committed to sailing it together their own course depends on it. They have created the *b'rith;* now its presence helps to create their future.

Jewish history posits the events at Sinai to have constituted a fundamental pact between God and the people. It is this event which makes Jewish history possible, this and this alone.

Several questions arise. How can one speak of God pacting with man, as if it were a contract between equals? Further, what is unique about Sinai? Further, is the Bible a true record of the encounter, as reliable as a comparable document in secular history? And why should the *b'rith* bind one who lives millennia later? I will take up these questions in order.

How can God speak with man, obligate man, and be obligated in turn? To him who knows the presence of the living God as a reality the answer is obvious. If ever one has experienced His presence in blinding flash or in the still small voice, one knows at once that He never merely is but that His being always makes demands. With infallible accuracy do the biblical writers reflect this truth. From Adam to Noah, from Abraham to Moses, from Amos to Jeremiah —the revelation of I Am is always followed at once by the inevitable Thou Shalt or Thou Shalt Not. An unrevealed God may be the philosopher's God, inferred, synthetized, and reasoned out, argued about and disputed. The revealed God is to him who has seen the Presence unarguable and always demanding. I may say No to His urging and like Jonah take flight, but if I say Yes I have made a covenant, have entered my own *b'rith* with Him. Long after the moment of divine insight has passed the obligation remains as does the fabric of love in which it is clothed. What formerly I might have done in clear choice is now shaded by the ought of the *b'rith*. The ought becomes *mitzvah*, the demand to do, for to know God's presence must also mean to know demand. The Jew has never felt that faith alone is enough. Without works it is barren. Hence Judaism knows no catechism which, if learned and believed, will make one a Jew in faith. Put differently, the I–Thou relationship of man and God, because it is relationship, touches on obligation.

The *b'rith* also speaks of God's obligation. For if revelation implies demand and demand means *mitzvah,* the caprice of God becomes an impossibility. What He sets as law to man He also sets as limit to Himself. Revelation is divine self-limitation as is the moral demand it draws in its train.

There is a passage in Psalms which served the ancients as foil for this truth. The Hebrew is ambiguous, but usually it is translated to read:

> For it is a law unto Israel,
> A statute of the God of Jacob.[3]

The Hebrew text, taken literally, should however make us render the second line as a true parallel to the first (which is the characteristic of Hebrew poetry) and understand it to say:

> A statute *unto* the God of Israel.

In that case, say the rabbis of old, the Psalmist conveys to us an insight of the interdependence of God's and man's law, and the verses, freely rendered, affirm:

> What is law unto Israel
> Is a statute to the God of Jacob.

In the realm of natural sciences this insight has long been accepted. He has created the physical laws of the universe and has thereby withdrawn His omnipotence from their execution. The same may be said of moral laws. They too delimit His power. It is in this sense that God can be said to be dependent on His creation, and in a special way on those to whom He has chosen to reveal Himself. The content of the demand touches both Him who issues and him who receives it. If He can say that "the *mitzvah* is not far from you,"[4] then He Himself must not be far away.

The historic reality of revelation is the foundation of Christianity and Islam. Both of these religions are founded on the confrontation of one man with the One God, of the God-man or prophet with the source of demand. There is nothing in my world view which would make me hesitate to ascribe the possibility of revelation to these two or in fact to all times and all men. To me, the reality of divine encounter between God and Jesus, Paul, or Mohammed is as plausible as the vision of Isaiah. Whether the records of such encounters are "true" or whether the consequences men drew from these records are also due my respect is another matter to which I will revert in a later chapter. But to believe that God revealed Himself only to my people would be preposterous. The biblical authors certainly did not give way to such self-adulatory conceit. They neither needed nor made an explanation for God appearing to Abimelekh or speaking to Balaam. They did claim that Moses' revelatory experiences marked him off from other prophets in that God spoke to him "face to face," but it was in length, repetition, and clarity that his relationship was said to differ, not in the nature of revelation itself.

THE REALITY OF SINAI

But Sinai was different. For while everywhere else in the sacred history of God and man it was the individual soul which opened itself to the Presence, *at Sinai it was a whole people. Therein lies the uniqueness of the moment.* It was, as no less a maker of human history than Winston Churchill once remarked, "the most decisive leap forward ever discernible in the human story."[5]

I use "Sinai" as a point in time and place without being able to fix either one exactly. "Sinai" may be a succession of moments or a single one, a succession of places or a single one. "Sinai" is an experience in the life of one people, a confrontation never achieved before or after, a whole people entering into a compact, and God therefore becoming forever entangled in the fate of this people. For the encounter gives rise to the *b'rith*, not another revelation with its demands on one to whom He speaks, but *the* single unequaled fate-ridden covenant with the People of the Covenant.

If this moment did not take place, Jewish history is fiction piled on fiction, the unusually tortuous tale of a people's suffering for the sake of nothing. If it took place it marks a watershed in time. A new dimension is added to history; a whole people who walk through history as any other "natural" people have added the quality of a "supernatural" people to their wondrous existence. They live forever after on two plains which are yet one and the same, exposed to men and nations with their demands and exposed to God with His.

One's own *b'rith* with the One Who Speaks makes its pressing weight felt in every single action. Prophetic experience is rare and its consequences are accounted shattering. But a whole people's *b'rith* made the sky of history red with the lightning of awe and the thunder of revelation so real that the people "saw" it—what an expressive way to describe the indescribable! How this came to be or why is a matter of biblical and post-biblical conjecture. That it did happen in a great single burst of spiritual reaching constitutes both the birth and the explanation of the riddle of the Jew. Here it was formed, here lies the gravitational point of its natural and supernatural history.

What precisely was revealed? The traditional answer that the written and oral Laws in their entirety were entrusted to Moses at Sinai is unacceptable to me. Only the written Law then? I rebel equally against this thought. The subsequent history of Israel is inconceivable if one assumes the Torah to have been its possession since Sinai. Besides, critical historic and archaelogical research have rendered so simplistic a view untenable. Much of the Torah is post-Sinaitic; how much is still in scholarly dispute.[6]

In every revelation the ex post facto contemplation of the experience is soon part of the experience itself. The consequences man draws become indistinguishable from the original demand. "This is what God wants me to do," is my necessary reaction, but at the very moment I say it I can no longer be sure that my own volition has not subtly mingled with the divine. It cannot be otherwise. For it is no different in human communication.

You speak to me and I hear you. What you say is, to you, clear and unambiguous. But the moment your word strikes my ear it is no longer yours alone, it becomes part of me, of my consciousness, my will and my ability, my understanding as well as my misunderstanding. Hearing is interpretation of words, inflections, meaning. The better I know the speaker the surer I can be of his intent; the less I know him the more uncertain will I be of my comprehension.

So it is with revelation, and so it must have been at Sinai. Perhaps Franz Rosenzweig comes closest to the truth when he says that revelation consisted not of words but rather of God revealing *Himself*. What followed thereafter was the glorious and painful searching out of His will, with Moses as chief interpreter and his generation and all the later generations of Israel forever engaged in the search. Rosenzweig illustrates his insight with a memorable comment on the Ten Commandments. God "came down"—that is essentially the extent of revelation; "And God spoke" is already interpretation, and so is "I am the Lord thy God who led thee out of Egypt. . . ." What God revealed of all of this was only revelation, that is, Himself. All else was human consequence, human understanding of the supreme moment.[7]

Yet it was more than that. For the Presence always implied command. The reality of "I am the Lord" was only the beginning; "Thou shalt" was the necessary—or shall I say, specifically Jewish—consequence. Sinai meant that Israel knew both the existence of the living God and at the same time that special demands were made by Him of this people as a people. What was demanded was clearly understood at times, less clearly at others. Torah is the result of the meeting, and the living Torah with its *mitzvot* (precepts) is forever after the starting point of all who would try to follow the divine command through the medium of the unique document.

What does this interpretation do to this biblical record? Does it not make it purely human?

Yes and no. Yes, insofar as the book is humanly composed and has various authors who wrote at various times. No—and I speak here primarily, though not necessarily exclusively, of Torah—insofar as the book explores the revelation, remembers it in the changing prisms of the centuries and truly believes that it still speaks out of that great moment and in consequence of it. Who can deny that much of this was accurately grasped and came close to God's will? The glory of the Bible is partly human and surely in part divine.

But often the memory failed. It must have failed, simply because even this people could not forever be sustained by the flash of truth. Else there would have been no golden calf, no idols, no injustice, no need for prophecy. In a memorable essay Martin Buber once commented on the story of Saul, Agag, and Samuel. Samuel, speaking in God's name, instructs King Saul to war on King Agag and, upon capturing him, to put him to the sword. There are other instructions, all of which Saul faithfully carries out, all except one. He spares Agag. For this humane act God—again speaking through Samuel—decrees stern punishment for Saul. He is to lose both his own life and his throne for having failed the divine decree. Says Buber: I think Samuel misunderstood God, for I do not believe that God wanted Saul to be other than humane.[8]

In this way I too see the Bible, and especially the Torah. Did God want Israel to exterminate the seven nations of Canaan? The Torah says so. I do not believe it. The authors sincerely thought that this was what the revelation implied. Even though I am so much further removed from the event I take the liberty to doubt the accuracy of their reading of the divine intent. For what they saw, they saw through the tensions and needs of their time, when war had its rules and taboos even as it has in our day. The same is true for slavery. However much our harmonists and apologists try to soften the blow and point to the undoubted elements of humanitarianism in the treatment of slaves, I will never believe that God wanted men to be slaves, either then or now. The biblical authors bespeak their own people's moral advance in a thousand ways, and not the least here, but this does not make the relevant biblical laws a part of the *b'rith*.

You will ask: If this be so, how do we know what is and what is not touched by God? If part of the Torah is true, which part is? And who is to decide?

This is a question every non-Orthodox Jew (or Christian, for he faces the same quandary) must meet sooner or later and meet squarely. I will return to it in a later chapter, for at this point its resolution does not touch my central point, namely, that I stand upon both the possibility and the reality of Sinai. To this the Torah testifies, perfectly at times, imperfectly at other times. And Jewish history testifies to it, for it is possible only because of it. Torah, Prophets, the rest of the Bible, Mishnah, Talmud, and all the centuries of thinking, writing, searching, doubting, and finding, all these were responses to, and therefore part of, that moment of moments when a whole people saw the Presence and heard the demand: "And you shall be unto Me a kingdom of priests and a holy people." God met His people, the people met their God, and what in later generations they wrote into their sacred scriptures was meant to explore the moment and expand it into history.

There remains one question, in a way the crucial one: Granted the confrontation at Sinai was unique and Israel uniquely obligated itself, does this obligation stretch unlimited into the future? Does the ancient Covenant bind me, a late and possibly unwilling descendant?

No man can be forced to serve God. He may unwittingly advance divine goals, even against his own desire, but his will remains free. The most deterministic of all rabbinic sayings concedes that while all is predestined by Heaven, man's relationship to God is exempted.[9] No, I *can* repudiate *my* part in the Covenant. How successful such repudiation will be and what psychological or other consequences it will have on me is another question. But I can say No and go my own way.

But short of such outright repudiation I remain bound. In other words, if I do not say No I have made an existential statement. For I, a Jew, am born into this covenantal relationship as surely as I am born into my family. I can walk out on my parents and deny all responsibility toward them. Still, I entered the world as their child; their genes and chromosomes have formed me, their history is my history. Similarly, I live as a citizen of a nation. Unless I repudiate the covenant of citizenship between the nation and me, I am bound by the country's fate, its obligations and its demands. I must pay the cost of the Covenant. I have the alternative of how I will pay it, willingly or unwillingly, meaningfully or haphazardly; this too will be explored in detail later on.

A Jew, by the very condition of his Jewishness, pays the continuing price of Sinai. If Jewishness remains his fate, Judaism remains the framework of his native spiritual existence, and God his partner. And therefore, as long as the people as a continuing organism in history keep alive the consciousness of Sinai, each Jew can find his roots. The *b'rith* was his father's, but it is his also. Each generation should regard itself as standing at Sinai, says the Passover ritual. This is no empty phrase; it is a challenge thrust before the doubting as well as the believing: "You are what you are. Accept yourself, fulfill your destiny by making the eternal potential the actuality of your life. You are a Jew. Therefore, live as one in depth and meaning as well as in name!"

The secularist Jew sees it both differently and similarly. He too sees the future demanding and beckoning, but the demands he beholds are different in scope and origin. He will find his way and often we will meet. The Jewish people are his concern as they are mine. He too accepts himself. He does it for his own sake or for the sake of Israel. I do it ultimately for God's sake and because I must.

HOW ODD OF GOD

A well-known jingle proclaims with tearful jocularity: "How odd of God to choose the Jews." To the historical improbabilities is added the suprahistorical mystery of the Covenant with this particular people. Why the Jews? Why not another nation? Jews have asked this question, as have others.

Tradition abounds with explanations which, cast in the mold of popular legend, often are bearers of deep spiritual quandaries.

God did offer the Covenant to other peoples, one legend goes. Each in turn asked the conditions, the demands, and each found one particular demand too harsh or contravening a national custom. Only the children of Israel accepted without inquiry. They first said: "All that the Lord has spoken, we will do," and only then: "We will listen (to

the demand)." It is a comment on the unconditional trust
with which Israel was ready to meet its destiny. No task
would be too hard if God was the partner. There was
apparently no other people thus disposed, the midrash says,
and who can gainsay that this was indeed the case?[10]

But does not the biblical account itself contradict this?
Does it not ascribe the Covenant to a divine promise made
to Abraham, Isaac, and Jacob? Yes and no. The merit of the
Fathers plays a role; it is, so to speak, the precondition.
Without the Fathers there would not have been a people
ready to give assent. But promise or no, it depended in the
end on the moment at Sinai. The people met their God on
the foundation of their past and in the crucible of their
present.

You will say that I evade the question and have in part
turned it back to Abraham. Well then, you ask, why would
God choose this man above all others?

I do not know. Was he alone ready, alone among all
men? Perhaps. Or was it simply a "caprice of God," which
pious men call "grace," that set Abraham aside? I rather
think both elements played their role, the readiness of God
and the readiness of man, just as at Sinai later, the readiness of a people. Physical evolution works along these
principles. New forms emerge slowly and then suddenly the
species leaps forward in spectacular advances. Might spiritual history not be described in similar terms?

We began this chapter with a statement of faith. In the
end, the mystery of existence touches the mystery of purpose. I know of no better way to describe this resolution
of the riddle than to repeat the words of a simple song. It
was composed by an eighteenth-century Hasidic rabbi, Levi
Yitzhak of the little town of Berdichev in Eastern Europe.
He was a passionate champion of his people and in this
song brings the plight of his brethren before God.

Good morning to You, Lord of the world!
I, Levi Yitzhak, son of Sarah of Berdichev,
  approach You with a legal matter concerning
  Your people of Israel.
What do You want of Israel?
It is always: Command the children of Israel!
It is always: Speak unto the children of Israel!

Merciful Father! How many peoples are there in the world?
Persians, Babylonians, Edomites!
The Russians—what do they say?
  Our emperor is the emperor!
The Germans—what do they say?
  Our kingdom is the kingdom!
The English—what do they say?
  Our kingdom is the kingdom!
And I, Levi Yitzhak, son of Sarah of Berdichev say:
  I shall not go hence, nor budge from my place
  Until there be a finish
  Until there be an end
  Of the exile.

But when he comes to the climax, shaking his fist at the Almighty, when he faces the awesome possibility of renouncing his allegiance, he shrinks back and proclaims this resignation in the age-old words of affirmation, which Jews proclaim in their daily prayers and in the hours of sorrow:

> *Yisgaddal v'yiskaddash sh'may rabbo* . . .
> Magnified and sanctified be His great name!

Sooner or later comes one's confrontation with acknowledgment or rejection, one's inevitable auto-da-fé. It involves the elusive will of God and one's own choice. Sooner or later one must make a choice—even the choice of saying "Yes" to God's choice.

There is an old legend among our people which tells of

the indecision of our forefathers at Sinai. They were not sure that they could or should take upon themselves the yoke of the law that God had proffered them. Perhaps they had a brief prophetic glimpse into a future laden with agony and suffering. They began to veer away from Moses and the One who had sent him. It was then, says a midrash, that God told them: "If you accept My Torah it will be well with you, but if you do not, I will pick up this mountain, turn it upside down like a kettle and bury you underneath."[11]

This story has always struck me as revealing a particularly cogent insight into that crucial moment of our history. At first glance the legend seems to vitiate the possibility of free choice. What kind of choice is it that offers you death as an alternative? But this is precisely what is meant to be conveyed. Once God has chosen, acceptance or refusal are severely limited in the presence of the supreme religious demand. The price of "No" is death.

Every man who has ever stood face to face with the secret demands of his life knows what this means. In their presence there is no escape save self-denial and self-destruction. It is the peculiar, perhaps unique fate of the Jews to have been faced with this ineluctable demand as a people.

CHAPTER IV

The Uncertain Mission

Nothing is but what is not.

Shakespeare
Macbeth

The solution to the eternal riddle will escape us if we disregard the suprahistorical element of Jewish fate, if in other words we fail to take into consideration the reality and the importance of choice. Without choice and thereby chosenness the Covenant is fleshless, and in turn, without the reality of God choice becomes meaningless, for where there is a choice there must be a chooser and a chosen.

THE CONCEPT OF CHOICE

The very term "Chosen People" makes many moderns recoil. It smacks of ugly feelings of superiority. It has a tinge of exclusiveness, it appears to be, to use Kaplan's term, an anachronism, a flight into the mystique of the supernatural —altogether unworthy of a self-respecting twentieth-century intellectual.

Perhaps—and then, perhaps not.

For the concept of choice which I view as the key to the riddle is not the chosenness of which my fathers conceived, nor is it the choice which Toynbee excoriates. The concept of chosenness has all too long been moored in stale and marshy thoughts. But there are other vistas which combine the landscape of old ideas with the excitement of contemporary insights.

We begin with Sinai and all it implies. We begin with a meeting of a people and its destiny. It is a two-sided event: God choosing His people, a people choosing its God. I will not deny that in the course of centuries and under the intolerable pressure of cruel neighbors this concept fostered among Jews a sense of superiority, an inverted defense against the yellow badge, with which the Christian sought to mark the Jew as an obviously inferior being.

It is true that, as the pressure grew, the feigned Jewish disregard of the environment grew into disdain, then contempt and even hatred. It was then that the Gentile became a *goy*, it was then that the universal elements in Judaism faded into the background and a self-protecting armor of self-glorifying chauvinism supported the crumbling framework of a faltering people.

It is true that over the centuries the idea of Jewish chosenness created a spiritual myopia, that ends and means, realities and dreams became inextricably intertwined. No wonder that when the spring of emancipation dissolved the encrustations of centuries, it broke also the shield which chosenness had been to its bearers. Even before the idea of chosenness was battered in the Hitlerian onslaught and singed with doubt, it had retreated from the consciousness of the people into the refuge of the prayer book and the study hall. Even before that, and certainly thereafter, the average Jew would no longer say, "I am a member of the Chosen People." He did not care to face either the imagined sneers of his Gentile fellow citizens, or the reality of his own disbelief.

Chosenness indeed! It smacked of a sense of arrogance, the very thing the Jew objected to when he met it among

Gentiles in his own economic and social struggles. Chosenness gave the lie to the egalitarian aspirations of the emancipated Jew. Had we not finally arrived—at least theoretically—at an acknowledgment of human equality? One could not strive for the ideal democratic society and still believe that "all are equal, but some more equal than others."

But a good deal of the excitement and eyebrow raising about chosenness was unnecessary. If there is a problem, it exists primarily because we continue to cherish an outmoded understanding of choice and chosenness, which was convenient and useful at one time, but which fails to meet our own needs or reflect our own understanding. Jewish exclusiveness and Jewish superiority are not the same as chosenness, even though the latter may produce the former. The concept of choice is thereby not invalidated.

Why is a Jew? Let there be no misunderstanding. *The Jew is what he is because of a double choice: because of his choosing and his being chosen, but the content of this choice, its meaning and its significance are not necessarily what the words have conveyed in the past.*

FROM ABRAHAM TO BABYLON

How did the idea develop and how did it reach its present spiritual impasse?

It is well to understand this concept thoroughly so that a new and dynamic approach may be built on its foundations.

The traditional Jewish and Christian views assign to the relationship between God and Israel an unchanging static quality. They say that at one moment in history God in His infinite wisdom chose for Himself a singular man, Abraham, and entered with him into a Covenant which stipulated that his descendants would become the chosen of God and as numerous as the sand by the sea. Their presence, their faith, their deeds would be a blessing to mankind. Slowly and often with tantalizing contradiction, the promise went forward to its climax at Sinai.

Abraham has no offspring, until Isaac becomes the gift of his old age. Next, the aged father is bidden to sacrifice this very gift, the bearer of the promise itself, and then is restrained from doing so. Through difficult years and generations the story sinks to the abyss of Egyptian slavery. From the depths of despair and with the promise all but forgotten by Israel, the people rise toward freedom and toward the moment of meeting with their God. And now at Sinai the prologue is over, the people exist. The message is given to Moses and transmitted by him. The curtain rises, the first act begins.

Now the people are sent forth to fulfill their task. There are advances and retreats. The people are not ready, a whole generation has to die in the desert before its descendants can face the all too mundane task of conquering the land of Canaan. Moses dies; Joshua and other judges in turn succeed him. The nation grows, but not always inwardly. It assimilates the customs and the knowledge of other peoples, but not always their best. It takes one step forward and sometimes two steps backward. Men arise to lead it out of its fate, toward an existence like that of other nations. A few men bar the way, attempt to press the people back on the road of mission: seers, prophets, preachers, priests, and all who retain a glimpse of the promise and the potential.

Imperceptibly the law takes form, the ancient rules are amplified and deepened, interpreted and adapted to changing circumstances. The first political catastrophe befalls the nation: its leadership is banished from the land, the Temple destroyed by the men from Babylon. At little meeting houses far away on the banks of the Tigris and Euphrates the spark of Torah is kept alive and the candle of promise kept burning. Israel now sees itself as the servant of God, the *Eved Adonai,* "despised and forsaken of men, a man of pains and acquainted with disease, as one from whom men hide their face . . ."[1] But this is not the end, for the promise retains its force and the prophet puts it into new words:

> Behold, My servant shall prosper
> He shall be exalted and lifted up,
> And shall be very high.[1]

In the second half of the sixth pre-Christian century they begin to return to the land, to new tasks, new opportunities, new difficulties, new wars, new challenges. The promise remains. Scribes and their successors, lay scholars called rabbis, develop the law and attempt to deepen the consciousness of the people, to the end that their entire existence might be devoted to the service of the Most High. There are parties and sects, even monastics: Pharisees and Sadducees, Essenes and brotherhoods; there are opportunists who flatter the Roman conquerors, and Zealots ready to give their lives for a successful revolution. A people like other people, a nation like other nations, then and later— yet also a nation unlike any other, for it still responds to the command and remembers the Word which so often becomes a burden.

THE BURDEN AND THE TASK

> Behold my servant, whom I uphold;
> Mine elect, in whom My soul delighteth,
> I have put My spirit upon him,
> He shall make the right to go forth to the nations.
>
> I the Lord have called thee in righteousness,
> And have taken hold of thy hand,
> And kept thee for a covenant of the people,
> For a light of the nation.

A light unto the nations! The missionaries begin to wander across the seas and lands. At the seats of the high and mighty, even in Rome, men turn to the faith of Abraham and Moses. Colonies of converts are established. Jews spread to all parts of the Mediterranean world, from Spain to Egypt (where great communities flourish and temples are built) and even to India, to China and inner Africa. In all the lands of his sojournings the Jew is bidden

> To open the blind eyes,
> To bring out the prisoners from the dungeon,
> And them that sit in darkness out of the prison house.
> I am the Lord, that is My name.[2]

When shall the task be done? The Lord will choose His time.

Meanwhile, Israel is a nation in waiting, readying itself for the day when it can accomplish what it had set out to do long generations ago. Meanwhile, it goes on the path God has hewed out for it, undeterred by setbacks and suffering, by frustration and disappointment. It observes the laws of old, it plumbs the meaning of Torah, it brings its precepts into the life of every day. Israel is a soldier who waits until its commander is ready.

There is no essential distinction between the traditional Christian and the traditional Jewish view, except that Christianity teaches that the mission has come to its end with the arrival of Jesus. It was this which constituted the fulfillment of the promise. The story had a beginning with Abraham and an end with Jesus. Isaiah's prophecies were fulfilled, the suffering servant was not Israel, but Jesus, son of Mary and son of God. He was the bruised reed "who by His knowledge did justify the Righteous One to the many."[3] The faithful of the emerging Christian church were the New Israel. In a way the story began all over again, the promise now waiting for its second fulfillment.

To the Jew the line that stretched from Abraham down to the present remained unbroken. Jesus was an incident in Jewish history but signified neither break nor fulfillment. His followers were at first considered schismatics and in the end apostates and therefore of no further concern to the people of God.

The elect of the Lord continued to wait. They had added Mishnah and Talmud to amplify and actualize the words of Torah, and generations of scholars labored to make the will of God accessible to new times, new ears, new hearts. The objective seemed to remain eternally the same: to be a light unto the nations.

"HOW LONG, O LORD?"

As the Jew retreated into mediaeval isolation, it became both easier and harder to maintain this faith in the ultimate fulfillment. Easier, because the surrounding world was so clearly mantled in darkness, in illiteracy and ignorance, while the Jew, despised of men, retreated to his hovels, there to learn, to write, to study, to expound, to philosophize—and to pray that God might not wait forever. In a way it was easier to maintain the belief in the unchanged mission, because of the contrast the Jew saw between his own spiritual world and the world without. But it was hard, too; waiting required untold deeds of heroism. The Jew cried: "How long, O Lord?" and he cried it with every fiber of his being, he cried it as he fled for his life, he cried it as he committed suicide, he cried it when he was burned at the stake. One cannot forever believe in a God who persists in waiting. The sin of His people, great as it might have been, could not have been so monstrous that it would justify centuries of agony, ignominy, and torture; there had to be some more immediate purpose, some more dynamic mission which needed fulfillment now, which was more than a spiritual holding operation, unspecified for an indeterminate future.

So, during the height of the Middle Ages and in the centuries thereafter, there reappeared the mystics with their books and their teachings, First came the Cabalists and then the pious ones called Hasidim. The source of all their spiritual drive was the belief that Israel need not wait forever for God; the deed worthy of salvation could be accomplished before the far-off days would come and could be brought to its magnificent realization at any time, even now.

Some said that if one knew the secret name of God or any of the mysteries of the universe, if one could acquire a knowledge of the alchemy of the spiritual world, the Day of the Lord could be brought closer.

Still others taught and believed that God was waiting for Israel, not Israel for its God. God could be reached by the rising soul of each Jew, who would ascend the *sefirot* (rungs) one by one. Man, as it were, could force the hand of God.

Others still felt that the promise would find fulfillment if enough Jews would carry out the will of God truly, as laid down in tradition, others if even one single human being could fully do the will of God. This faith found its apotheosis in the story of a young child attempting to keep the Sabbath completely and faithfully, for, so he had been told, were he able to do so the Messiah would come.

There was a mingling now of present tasks and eschatological hopes. It was no longer, as heretofore, Israel that would lift the prisoners out of the dungeon, but God's servant, the Messiah, would come at the end of days and lead Israel back to the land of its fathers and fulfill the ancient promise of God. At the end of days! There was a bitter pessimism in this pious affirmation, which postponed the execution of Israel's task into the post-historical era.

For if God's promise would not be carried out until His Anointed would come, what was Israel's task in the meantime? Merely to be? Merely to wait until it could be a blessing to the nations? There were attempts to break through the iron circle that such a concept of chosenness imposed upon the people. There was above all the ever present belief that God needed continual witnesses. In the moment of supreme trial a Jew would lay down his life for the sanctification of God's name. This all too often repeated act of supreme testimony came to be known as *kiddush ha-shem.*[4]

There were some who went even further, who believed that Israel was literally upholding the existence of the world. A tradition developed which said that at any given moment in history there were thirty-six men alive, thirty-six righteous ones (most said thirty-six Jews, but there was no unanimity on this) who by their being, by their pure lives, by their knowledge of God, by their righteousness, by their very existence made possible the continuation of man. Without them mankind would sink into sin, suffering would lose its meaning, and faith would break on the rocks of cynicism. If this was so, then these thirty-six pious ones were indeed reason for the continued existence of Israel. Then the nation would have more than the task of waiting: it would have a dynamic mission to provide the thirty-six. But the theory of the *lamed-vavniks* (so-called after the Hebrew letter symbols for 36) was too speculative to make an observable dent in the consciousness of the people. How could one believe that a people existed for the sake of the thirty-six, and the thirty-six for the sake of man—especially since no one had ever seen them? It was belief piled upon faith, it was mysticism driven to its furthest point, and upon this no people could long persist. But, and this must be stated, it was an attempt to give dynamic character to the static and stubborn concept of Israel's chosenness.[5]

The moment the ghetto gates creaked open and the Jew began to leave his not-so-splendid isolation, the problem of his fate and purpose in the world was given new urgency. The answer of the mystics and the Hasidim or the theory of the *lamed-vavniks* simply would not do for men and women who were acquiring a universal education. Why were Jews in the world? What was it they were called upon to maintain? Were they still waiting for the end of days?

The nineteenth-century Reformers had the courage to break into the mired undergrowth of chosenness. If they too did not succeed in their quest, at least they tried to give new meaning to the ancient idea.

They went back to Isaiah. If Israel was to be a light unto the nations, this was surely meant to be a constant task, not one postponed to the end of days. The mission of Israel, they held, was not accomplished in waiting, and holding the fort for God, but in being visibly, courageously, and constantly the finest examples of a God-intoxicated people.

"It is the destiny of Judaism," said Samuel Holdheim, preacher of the Reform Association in Berlin toward the middle of the last century, "to pour the light of its thoughts, the fire of its sentiments, the fervor of its feeling, upon all souls and hearts on earth. Then all of these people, the nations, each according to its soul and historic characteristics, will, by accepting our teachings, kindle their own lights, which will then shine independently and warm their souls. Judaism shall be the seed-bed of the nations, filled with the blessing and promise. It is the Messianic task of Israel to make the pure knowledge of God and the pure law of the morality of Judaism the common possession and blessing of all the peoples of the earth. We do not expect of the nations that, by accepting these teachings, they would give up their historic characteristics in order to accept those of our people; and similarly we shall not permit the Jewish people to give up its innate holy powers and sentiments so that it might be assimilated among the nations.

"This, then is our task: to maintain Judaism within the Jewish people and at the same time to spread Judaism among the nations; to protect the sense of Jewish unity of life and faith without diminishing the sense of unity with all men; to nourish the love for Judaism without diminishing the love of man."[6]

THE HARSH REALITIES

It was a splendid thought, generous, inspiring, and visionary, but it too had little relation to the harsh realities of the contemporary world. It was an ancient thought dressed in modern garb; it was a new name for an old goal. It supplied no new substance. It too did not say how the mission would be accomplished; it too spoke of a light unto the nations, but failed to say what kind of light. It spoke of example, but did not say how such an example should be given. It was nobility dressed in the cloak of vagueness. It created at first a sentimental enthusiasm, which in the very nature of things was followed by disappointment and frustration when the age of fulfillment refused to come into sight.

For here the modern liberal and his more traditional forebears parted ways: while the latter had been satisfied to postpone the fruits of chosenness until the days of the Messiah and were meanwhile willing to take upon themselves the yoke of the law with all it implied, the new liberal Jew looked for a more immediate harvest. No ultimate postponement would do for him. To be sure, he too believed that the complete brotherhood of man would come only at the end of time; still, men could meanwhile set out together on the road and Israel could take them by the hand.

Alas, mankind failed to move and Israel failed to lead;

the "light unto the nations" began to sputter and burn lower and lower. The idea of mission continued to haunt liberal textbooks and theological treatises and for some decades was standard content for sermons. When the twentieth century got under way, Jewish liberalism was precisely where it had been when it left the ghetto one hundred years before. In the "mission of Israel" it had acquired a new vocabulary for chosenness, but not an essentially new thought about it. It was still the same concept and the same resignation to postponement, only now the faith was not as strong, the willingness to suffer not as keen, for naturalism had begun to erode the sturdy faith, and further deterioration was inevitable.

In time mission and chosenness became embarrassing ideological ballast. They were either played down or denied altogether. In some prayers in the new Reform ritual the phrase, "Thou hast chosen us from amongst all nations" was omitted. In others it was maintained in the Hebrew, but transmuted into softer language in the translation. Chosenness now was identified by some with chauvinism and anti-egalitarianism. Where the thought persisted it lost its force. Finally came the tragedy of the six million, which seemed to make hollow mockery out of the ancient phrase. A chosen people indeed! Where would it lead the nations? Into gas ovens and mass graves?

Not even the new State of Israel could resuscitate the thought of chosenness, for the religious aspect of its rebirth paled before its national and human significance. Now Jews when they sought refuge had a place to go. Now there were men and women willing to embrace them as their brothers. If there was any connection between David ben Gurion and David the son of Jesse it was not clear. There were probably more Christian fundamentalists than Jews who believed that the re-establishment of Israel was the expression of God's love in fulfillment of the ancient covenants.

And so the mission, the chosenness, remained in limbo, suspended between the promise of old and the dreams of tomorrow. The promise had not changed and if one chose to believe, one would have to continue to wait—perhaps forever.

Here I take my stand. *I cannot believe that waiting is in itself and of itself the content of the Why of Jewish history.* It is of course conceivable, but my flesh and my heart rebel against such pietistic faith. My eye surveys the centuries and beholds the present, and what I see is not constancy but change. God may be constant. His tasks are not. I think I see His writing upon the turning pages of history. I would be less than human if I were not tempted to look more closely, to see whether I perchance might decipher the changing script. "The changing script"—perhaps here, in the kaleidoscopic light of dynamic history, we Jews can read new messages, and *discover that there is more than one Why to our existence.*

DYNAMIC MISSION

Is there a relationship anywhere which has the blood of life coursing through it, yet does not change and forever remains the same? It is inconceivable. When a messenger is engaged by his employer, will the message which he is to deliver be always and unvaryingly the same? The permanence of marriage, the constancy of affection between parents and children, the abiding loyalty of friends, are these not forever shifting in content to meet the moods and needs of changing years? Does growth not alter all of us? Two parties covenant for life to perform their tasks in an expanding or contracting and always renewing world. The covenant may stand, but neither its needs nor its deeds that give it substance will remain what they were at the beginning. So it is also with Israel, the messenger, and the Employer with whom he covenanted long ago.

My fathers believed in a living relationship between them and their fathers' God. With them I believe in the reality of a Sinai constantly renewed. It alone makes plausible and necessary my continued existence as a Jew, for nothing else will.

But I also believe that the tasks which Moses faced were not those of his forebears, nor were they his descendants' tasks, nor are they the same as mine. When Isaiah or Jeremiah said "Thus saith the Lord," they spoke to their contemporaries out of the exigency of *their* time. I readily repeat their words and seek to apply their inspiration and their universal truths, but my time is not their time and I cannot simply use their words to transplant the reality of a bygone age into the acuity of mine and say with confidence, "Thus saith the Lord also today." *If the Lord speaks today, He will speak to the burning issues of our time.* We stultify both the relevancy of our faith and the urgency of the religious demand if we fence them in the corral of yesterday's concerns. The rehearsal of yesterday's message can be guide and inspiration for today, but each generation must strain to listen to the still small voice in its own time.

The Sinaitic covenant determines, so to speak, the terms and outlines of Israel's employment. It sets forth direction but does not predetermine the changing content of the work that must be done.

Saying Yes to chosenness is possible today because it does not mean that there was or is only one mission. *Rather, there are many missions, varying tasks, changing from age to age, from need to need.* The Jew in Spain may have believed that he carried his torch for the same reason as did the Jew in Poland, but it was not the same torch. The twentieth-century descendant of the Patriarchs faces tasks peculiarly his own. I see a mission filled with the dynamism of life, growing, receding, growing again, thrusting forth in one direction, then in another. The Servant of the Lord still labors in the hazardous, changing service of his Master, who requires of him the ever new.

ETERNAL UNCERTAINTY

If then the mission has changed, if it was different in many yesterdays and different today and will yet be new tomorrow, what has it been, what is it, what will it be? Here surely must lie the answer to the riddle. Here at last the Why of Jewish existence is uncovered and exhibited to view.

Yet, as the vision opens before our eyes, a mist of uncertainty arises to cover it, for if, as we posit, the essence of the Why consists in a unique relationship between Israel and its fate, between the human and the divine, then to pretend that the meaning of such a relationship can be clear and unambiguous is to be pretentious or presumptuous, or both. Where is the man who can say with certainty that he can read the many *mene tekels* and know their meaning? Where is the man who can trace with surety what the finger of God has written? Even among those of our historians whose sense of the religious is kept strictly outside the gates of their craft, there is no unanimity about the meaning of purely *human* history. (This uncertainty is in fact a good thing, for it provides us with an infinite variety of speculative insights into the dynamics of the human story.) And if we add to this complexly woven fabric the stipulation of meaning which goes beyond the purely human realm, which seeks its foundation beyond the process of history itself, we have added thereby not clarity but further questions. The possibility of the divine-human encounter in personal and suprapersonal existence *adds the*

element of uncertainty, not of certainty. It adds the last
question to the others already asked or likely still to be
asked. *The only certainty I have is my uncertain apprehension of the truth.* I see it and see it clearly, but I know
that I behold only a part. I may attempt to penetrate to
the core, but whatever knowledge I may garner must be
prefaced by the great "perhaps." This "perhaps" is the human safeguard against arrogance in science as in philosophy. In science it distinguishes the true scientist—who
knows that he is but theorizing and surmising, probing and
testing—from the small mind whose narrow limits will admit nought of the overwhelming possibilities of an un-
charted, unknown realm of being and knowledge. So too
it is in our understanding of history: we must forever be
uncertain, we may surmise, but we cannot know with sure-
ness.

If this be true for the study of human history it is forever
true in Jewish history. The Covenant has meaning and substance. It is the foundation of meaning. Its fundamental
Why is the source of both certainty and uncertainty. Its
content may be sought and perchance it may be glimpsed,
but never in its last and farthest reaches.

I will go further and say that *it is the nature of the Jew
to know that his existence is grounded in meaning but that
the changing meanings of his passing days will forever be
withheld from him.* It is an old problem which confronted
Israel even before Sinai. "We shall not know with what to
worship the Lord until we arrive there," Moses said to
Pharaoh, and we still say it today.[7] We are messengers and
at times the message seems clear enough. At other times
again, the yoke it imposes and the task of which we are
to be the bearers are incomprehensible. The changing nature of the challenge keeps us forever wondering about ourselves and the One who sent us. "Judaism," Leo Baeck once
said, "is readiness for God."[8]

To be a Jew then means to be certain about the Why of being and uncertain about its daily significance. It is knowing and not knowing, it is asking questions for which the answer cannot be established. This is not to say that in fact there are no answers to the questions. It is to say, however, that we are doomed—or privileged, it depends upon the way we look at it—to be eternally uncertain about the place we occupy and the road which stretches ahead. Jewish existence, much like human existence, hypothesizes the question and the search. The Jew knows he is sent, he listens to the message, yet he must know that in the end there is the great "perhaps."

THE KEY WORD "PERHAPS"

It is the nature of Jewish existence to be wrapped in uncertainty. It is its existential quality. It is part of its burden to trust the meaning of its fate. "Perhaps" is the key word of the Jewish existence. *We say perhaps to the meaning of the moment, but—and this is central—not to meaning itself.* We may not know the purpose of today's mission, but we believe that the mission exists. To put it differently: we know there is a script, though we may not be able to decipher it with clarity.

I read the pages of Jewish history and I see not only existence but also direction. I see the event and I think I glimpse the mission. Still, even now, after centuries have passed, I am not sure, and I must therefore preface my understanding with "perhaps." I do it not out of well-mannered modesty; I do it from the conviction that Jewish meaning cannot be described otherwise.

Perhaps it was the task of Abraham to bring the knowledge of the one God, supreme, demanding, omnipotent, to the children of men. Abraham is man emerging into the sunlight of spiritual understanding, struggling, torn, tragic at times like all great figures, but blessed with the hope that new vistas were open and that what he had begun, his children and his children's children might carry on.

Perhaps it was the meaning of enslavement in Egypt to demonstrate the possibilities of redemption. Never before had slaves been set free en masse. Henceforth, wherever and whenever men were oppressed they could see visions of liberation and dream of freedom. Ever since, through the millennia, men have cherished the dream. In strange succession the American white revolutionaries saw their struggle in the light of the biblical Exodus (the first seal of the United States showed the parting of the Red Sea), and less than a century later, during the American Civil War, the Negroes thought of themselves as the children of Israel in Egypt. White and black dreamt the dreams of the eternal people, their language was the language of Moses and Aaron, their cry the unceasing cry of the oppressed. To them, as to their spiritual antecedents, there was a Promised Land of freedom which beckoned in the distance. Perhaps here as nowhere else the uncertain or even unfulfilled nature of meaning, unfettered by time-bound events, stands out against the darkling horizon of questions, because the content of mission for which we search may not fully be revealed until many centuries have passed.

Perhaps it was the role of the Prophets to expand the vision of Israel's God to the four corners of the earth, to bring the possibility of universal justice and universal concern into the realm of human comprehension. Or perhaps it was the juxtaposition of might and right, of power and principle, which formed the content of their mission: a Nathan confronting David, an Elijah upbraiding Ahab, an Amos thundering at Beth El, a Jeremiah railing against the establishment from the dank corners of his dungeon. Perhaps it was the meaning of Jewish existence in those centuries to engender and keep alive such revolutionary thoughts, to lay the foundations of freedom in the final, in the supreme sense.

Perhaps in the age of the Greeks it was the task of the Jew not only to keep alive the concept of moral possibility and moral demand, but also to synthetize it with the Greek ideal, to open the vision of a world in which Hebrew and Greek might be at one. Of the new world concepts the stubborn resistance of the Jew made possible, Christianity was surely not the least.

For *perhaps* it was the Jewish task to bring forth not only Hillel but Jesus, to be parent to the Christian faith so that in turn the world view of Judaism might touch the hundreds of millions whom Judaism itself would never reach. Twelve hundred years later at the height of the Middle Ages, Maimonides so conceived of Christianity's role, but he did so mainly to deny that Christians and Moslems were idolaters. I would go on from there and clearly say that I too see Jesus as divinely willed. That is to say, I see Christianity as more than a historic accident, another factor of human development. I see Christianity entering the realm of Jewish mission, so that perhaps it was the content of chosenness in that portentous age to bring forth Jesus. We will have more to say on this matter later on.

No less and no more I would say about Islam, for it too is ultimately a child of the Hebrew Bible and of the Jewish spirit though removed from its immediate context by time and circumstance. Yet its rise, too, is perhaps part of our chosenness, it too divinely willed and wanted.

Perhaps during the Middle Ages it was the content of Jewish chosenness to be the bridge between East and West, between Islam and Christendom. Jews were the purveyors of fructifying thought; they spoke Arabic and they also spoke the languages of Europe. Jews communicated with each other across cultural borders which to others were high and impenetrable walls. They studied the mathematicians of the East and the scholastics of the West. Perhaps it was they who were meant to be the catalysts of the Renaissance. Without them the rebirth of modern culture might not have come to pass in the way it did. "It was the Wandering Jew who bore westward the magic draught."[9]

And *perhaps,* too, it was they who in a way made possible the Christian Reformation. For it was the study of Hebrew, the rediscovery of Jewish sources, which spurred the drive toward the purification of an encrusted Christian tradition. Zwingli was a fine Hebraist and composed a commentary on part of the Old Testament in the tradition of the rabbis; Michael Servetus, the anti-trinitarian reformer, died because of his "Judaizing" tendencies; Reuchlin and Calvin were accused of having yielded too greatly to Jewish religious views.[10] Luther had Hebrew teachers and, as we mentioned before, who knows but that one of his central motivating powers, at least in the beginning, was the hope to win the Jews for Christ. "They are blood-relations of our Lord," he said once, "therefore, if it were proper to boast of flesh and blood, the Jews belong to Christ more than we. I beg, therefore, my dear Papists, if you become tired of abusing me as a heretic, that you begin to revile me as a Jew."[11] The Jew's presence in the midst of a Catholic Europe brought strange but powerful consequences for the renewal of a faith alien to him. This led a well-known student of this aspect of history to conclude: "The goal of Christian scholars for the use and study of the Hebrew language, the tendency to revolt from the complex system of Catholic theology to the seeming simplicity of Jewish dogmas, the effort to recover for the Bible its former centrality in Christian life, were a few of many indications of a Judaizing motif in the Reformation."[12]

It was this same Hebraic Puritan strain which gave character to the North American settlement. Leaving aside the minority influence of French-Catholic culture, the American continent bears the indelible imprint of the Hebrew Bible. Puritanism is Christianity in its Hebrew garb; Hebrew mortar, it was said, cemented the foundations of America. The first settlers spoke of themselves as "Christian Israel"; England was their Egypt, Charles I their Pharaoh, the ocean their Red Sea, and America their New Canaan, their Promised Land. Hebrew was required for a Bachelor's degree in seventeenth-century Harvard and Yale, and to this day the insignia of Yale University are Hebrew words in Hebrew script. Jews were few in colonial days, but their spiritual influence and the influence of the literature they had kept alive and pure were of surpassing significance.

And *perhaps* it was the very presence of the Jew, his existence in Western Europe, that loosed the first wave of emancipation, for it was around him that the controversy swirled in the beginning. It was of him that Abbé Grégoire and Mirabeau spoke and wrote. When the French National Assembly debates the rights of the Jews, the advocates of the old order sought to grant them toleration rather than rights, for they wanted no diminution of the prerogatives of the "dominant religion." It was then that Mirabeau mounted the rostrum and thundered:

"Dominant Religion! May these tyrannical words disappear entirely from our legislation. For if you allow this term in the realm of religion, you will have to allow it everywhere else: you will then have not only a dominant religious cult but also a dominant philosophy and a dominant system. No. Justice alone shall dominate; the highest principle is the right of the individual. All else must be subordinate to it."[13] It was the Jew's presence which bestirred the advocates of freedom to enlarge their call and to encompass all men in its demand. The French revolutionary spoke for the Jew and meant Man; the American revolutionary thought of himself as Jew and meant Man; the Negro thought of himself as Jew and meant Man.

Who can fathom the meaning of history to which we are so close, the extent of its tragedy and the depth of any meaning? Here surely all certitude must be muted, all brash assertion disdained. We will have occasion later to speak of the holocaust and of Israel rejuvenated. But even here the uncertainty of the mission's content cannot obliterate the certainty of its existence.

What then might it be today? I look at the world and I look at the Jew. Despite all its political diversity and the persistence of force and struggle, I see a world drifting toward ever increasing conformity of spirit, habit, thought, and behavior. I see the Jew desperately maintaining his identity, often without apparent purpose, often instinctively, almost intuitively. Often he is ignorant of his past and ignorant even of the possibilities of meaning that his present might hold for him. Often he merely exists, yet here too he may be serving a purpose beyond himself. For in the sea of conformity he may be the rock of difference. *Perhaps it is the destiny of the Jew today to maintain the possibility of minority and diversity.* He does it both willingly and unwillingly, at the price of disparagement and always at the cost of loneliness, but he is driven toward being himself even despite himself. And though, lacking both perspective and certitude, we venture to read the divine script, may we not here perhaps, in the contemporary conformity-diversity syndrome, find a clue to the Why of Jewish existence today?

Jews want to be part of the world yet they are driven to be separate. This was their fate in ages gone by, sometimes by choice, more often by force, and in time it became an ineluctable aspect of Jewish existence. Holiness forever tends toward separateness. *Kadosh* means holy, sanctified, and thereby that which is to be *kadosh* is set apart. "The people cannot come up to Mount Sinai," Moses reminds God at the crucial moment, "for You warned us, saying, 'Set *bounds about the mountain and make it* ka-dosh.'"[14] The mountain remained apart, and so, in history, did the people who assumed the holiness of that experience. Is it not possible then that those Jews who preach complete isolation from the environment may be close to the demand which is made by us today? May not separateness, resolute, exclusive aloneness be the mission of the Jew today as it has been—so it is said—in ages past?

It is possible, yet I read the changing script differently. I read it to tell of a people in the midst of other nations, who are, as Karl Barth once suggested, "a people that is no people—or perhaps no people who are a people after all."[15] Perhaps this is their task today: to be acculturated yet not assimilated; to be totally in this world yet also beyond it; to be loyal nationals of many countries yet the earth's true internationalists; to be the bearers of many cultures yet never to be known by them; to be acceptable yet never quite accepted, for *kadosh* is invisibly engraved on the forehead of every Jew.

Or *perhaps* it is our task today as Jews to be the bearer of social ideals, a whole nation providing social ferment in every corner of the globe. Perhaps it is the demand of our day—dimly grasped by some—that we be the champions of justice for others, not for ourselves. In the past the dread of persecution fastened chains of insecurity about our necks; we looked to ourselves and our needs and had no time for others. We asked "Is it good for the Jew?" and if it was we could say with clear conscience that it was good for the world also. We quoted Disraeli, who said, "The Lord deals with the nations as the nations deal with the Jews," and quoted history to prove in fact that whenever the Jew fared well in any society his hosts fared well also, and that whenever the Jew was in trouble so was the nation in whose midst he lived. The Jew, we said, was the barometer of the world's health and he was justified therefore to look to his welfare and security first and foremost.

But perhaps today the order of preference may be reversed. Perhaps today we ought to be that unlikely group in society that says, "What is good for others is good for us also"; that asks, "Is it good for man?"

Might a whole people see in this the core of its contemporary mission? Might a whole people make social justice or the establishment of international law the purpose of its striving? Might it so read the Book of Life in our time?

Or will the improbability of Jewish history be enriched by yet another unlikely chapter? Perhaps we ought to look for the improbable. *Perhaps today's uncertain mission lies where we would least expect it.*

We are not today a consciously spiritual people. Quite the contrary, we exhibit many discouraging signs of devotion to grossest materialism. In the land of Israel as elsewhere in the world the majority of our people give scant attention to the presence of any religious demand. Yet may precisely this be the unlikely content of our mission: to bring forth in this age a new religious message, a new fervor of extraordinary intensity? Is it for this that Israel was preserved and the exiles gathered into their national home? Once, when our softly cruising ship was approaching Mount Carmel in the starlit night, Martin Buber said: "Where but in Israel are the heavens so close that one might almost touch the stars?" Out of that land vast spiritual nourishment has in the past come to the world. Might it not happen again? Is it for this we live today? To keep alive the sparks of holiness among our people so that in the improbable moment it might ignite the consuming flame of faith?

Or is it perhaps our task today to insist on the possibility of divine grace in a world that denies the incursion of the divine? Is it possibly our task to insist on chosenness merely because it avows what man wants so strongly to disavow, to be the contrary element in a spiritually arid age? "Why do we dislike it so much," said Barth, "when we hear it said that the Jews are the Chosen People? Why do even Christians always look for new proofs that it is no longer so? Simply because we don't want to hear that the glory of free Grace, in which alone one can live, shines not here on us but on them, that not the Germans, French, Swiss, are chosen, but of all people the Jew! And consequently, if one wants to be chosen oneself one has to become, like it or not, a Jew or walk with the Jews in complete solidarity. 'Salvation comes from the Jews.'"[16]

Perhaps—or perhaps the mission lies somewhere else. We read the clues or misread them; they speak of today, not of yesterday or tomorrow. For us, it is today that makes its demand. We are obliged to seek its meaning, for man can never be himself unless he searches out the roots of his being and the possibilities of meaning. But once he glimpses his potential, once he envisions himself as a meaningful part of life's endless opportunities, then the vision becomes the man. Then he must act upon that which he understands, then even "perhaps" becomes an obligation. For the Jew there is none other.

Why is a Jew? The answer is fraught with existential uncertainty and with conditioned demands. The chief demand is to search and, having searched, to do. When we have done, we still cannot be sure. We can be sure only of our intent and of the knowledge that we can do no less. To the Jewish people above all applies the ancient adage found in the Ethics of the Fathers: "It is not given unto you to finish the task, but neither are you free to desist from it altogether."

CHAPTER V

A People Alone

> Why is Israel likened to an olive?
> Because even as olive oil cannot be
> mingled with other substances, so
> Israel cannot be mingled with other
> peoples.
>
> Midrash
> *Exodus Rabba*

There is an oft-quoted saying among Jews: *S'iz shvayr tsu zayn a Yid*—"It's hard to be a Jew." A sigh, touched by a tear, and accompanied by an existential shrug: So, what can you do about it? But the sigh remains, as does the tear.

If there was once a fierce pride in belonging to the Chosen Ones, it has been badly diluted today. In fact, most of our Jewish contemporaries would gladly jettison the whole idea. They feel self-conscious about it, even if they admit that the concept had reality and worth in days gone by. But not today.

Every year, when I begin to teach my Confirmation class, I ask them to react to the expression "Chosen People." Inevitably the vast majority of our sixteen-year-olds indicate a strong dislike for the term and what they think it means. They want no part of chosenness. Why? They usually present me with two reasons, one commendable and one, at least from my point of view, regrettable.

The commendable reason has to do with their sense of democratic equality. "We are all human beings," they say, "none better and none worse." In this sense chosenness offends them, and they believe it offends others. When I acquaint them with the writings of Mordecai M. Kaplan on this subject, they heartily agree with him.

In his chef d'oeuvre Kaplan has dealt with the whole matter at great length and with considerable passion. "The Chosen People Idea An Anachronism" is the title of a chapter in which he diagnoses those who still hold on to such outmoded thoughts as potentially suffering from maladjustment. "The idea of Israel as the Chosen People must, therefore, be understood as belonging to a thought world we no longer inhabit. . . . The very notion that a people can for all time be the elect of God implies an epic or dramatic conception of history, a history predetermined in form and aim. Nowadays for any people to call itself "chosen" is to be guilty of self-infatuation."[1]

THE BURDEN OF CHOICE

From the basically humanist position—which is the platform Kaplan occupies—this argument makes sense. If the "choice" is self-proclaimed and nothing more than that, then indeed it borders on either arrogance or delusion or both. If only man is involved in the choosing and not God, then there is much to commend Kaplan's suggestion that we shift from Israel's assumed chosenness to a self-assumed voluntary religious avocation. But this is where my reading of history diverges sharply from the humanist position. If, as I believe, the choice was *not* merely ours, the question of anachronism and delusion dissolves into meaninglessness —even though such concepts may admittedly lead to occasional afflictions of conceit and maladjustment and in fact have done so from time to time. We have to guard against this, of course, yet at the same time we must recognize that however awkward the whole idea may be, it belongs in the ineluctible framework of Jewish existence. *God is an awkward and awful predicament for the Jewish people.*

It is unquestionably easier to forget about the historic commission. To the majority of the Jews in the Diaspora it has become a burden, a yoke of embarrassment and guilt. Toward the outside world they would like to turn the tender cheek of equality—hoping to be accepted as equals because they themselves eschew all pretense of inequality. We once rejected you Gentiles, they say, but we do no longer. We kept apart not only because you forced us to live apart but because we wanted to. The urge no longer exists. Quite the contrary: we want to be part and partners of the whole fabric of life, from business to politics, from the fine and the social arts to the arts of fine and social living. "We have chosen to be unchosen," is the silent chorus of the Jewish middle classes in the Western world. They make every effort to wipe out their distinctiveness, they strive to be undistinguished.

"THE VANISHING JEW"

And they are succeeding only too well. They live better physically, and more poorly spiritually. They build fine communal institutions, because this is what Jews are supposed to do, yet they do not use them properly. They create and belong to splendid synagogues, and treat them as mausoleums. Jews are the least worshipful of any of the major groups identified with a religious background. Their attendance at services is so shockingly low that even the most courageous critics are afraid to face the facts. In medium-sized communities fewer than 10 per cent of those who are affiliated and identified with a synagogue will be in regular attendance, to say nothing of the many others outside the Temple gates. In larger cities the picture is darker still. The vaunted great Jewish revival has increased budgets and buildings and has created a slight stir of communal conscience. The intellectuals are absent; the college youth and young married people are absent; even the philanthropists and activists, the doers and drivers are absent. Rabbis preach to and castigate the few who are willing to listen and who need it the least.

It is not difficult to deepen the sense of gloom. New statistics show the rapid increase in mixed marriages. In some communities the rate has reached 50 per cent, as in Washington, D.C., and even in Canada where Jews appeared less prone to follow the trail of assimilation, the eastern and western provinces approach similar disintegration percentiles. "The Vanishing Jew" was not only the title of a widely debated article[2]; it was the long and somber shadow of a new threat. In suffering and pain the Jew had stood his ground. In freedom he seems to choose his own demise.

The unlikely hero of Jewish history now adds yet another chapter to the improbable story. The modern Jew of the Diaspora has all the ingredients of his contradiction-ridden ancestors.

He is free to live a Jewish life, and he strives to eschew it.

He is free to fill his spirit with all the treasures of the world, and he omits the treasures of his own tradition.

He fights for free religious expression and when he obtains it he forgoes its benefits.

He wants state and church separate so that he may not be encumbered in his religious particularity. When he wins his case he has nothing he wishes to be particular about.

He proclaims the home, rather than the school, as the

sanctuary where the spirit should be nurtured, yet his home is devoid of the searching, prayerful spirit.

He chooses to live near other Jews, he often sends his children to receive a Jewish education, yet he is distressed about the high cost of separateness. So that the synagogue may not fall into shame and disrepair, the member has to be assessed his dues and pressed to keep them in line with his financial capacity. No synagogue to my knowledge has yet had the courage to allow the Christian custom of voluntary contribution. We wouldn't dare. We bank on the magic attraction of the High Holy Days to bludgeon people into fulfilling their obligations. We sell tickets and withhold them from our financial recalcitrants. Only those who pay together pray together.

Even the voluntarism of philanthropy is more apparent than real. Especially in the higher brackets of giving, pressure by status associates tries to achieve what charity cannot. Jews are not alone in this, but the fact that misery has companions does not for long allay the pain. Now that the concentration and detention camps have closed and such terms as KZ and DP have disappeared from public parlance, now that Israel is beginning to stand more securely on its young legs, now that the utter urgency to give has lessened and the tears of compassion have dried, the receipts are fewer while the costs are rising.

And lest you think that this is the picture in America only, let me call on an astute observer of the Jewish scene overseas. "Gloomy Report from Europe," he entitles his piece, written in 1964. It is replete with quotations, polls and interviews from many countries; it contains such desperate assessments as: "We are dragging along. Maybe we're finished" (this one from England). Or: "Our Jews here are well-to-do. They give to drives and appeals. But they don't read and don't care about the Jewish future. All they want is to be left alone" (this from Belgium). "It is

clear," concludes the author, "that European Jewry is going through a process of spiritual decline. Temporarily?
Permanently? Who knows?"[3]

Are such the people chosen by God? As crazed by the
lures of comfort as their neighbors, would they not be in
truth exposing themselves to ridicule if they insist on the
ancient distinction? And if they say, in word and deed: "We
do not want the choice," can they walk away from it? Can
there be, to use the terminology of international affairs, a
unilateral repudiation of the Covenant?

Before I attempt to answer, let me point out the obvious,
namely, that I have spoken of the Diaspora. When the
answer is given it must include the Jews in Israel as well.
Where then do the latter stand on this question?

THE JEW IN ISRAEL

Israel has undoubtedly a larger share of believers in the
Covenant than any of the Jewish communities in the Diaspora, certainly in the Western Diaspora. The unique environment of the Holy Land encourages a significant appreciation of one's self as a Jew, and one's role in the divine
economy. The endemic and destructive self-hatred so often
found among Jews in the dispersion is happily absent. In
Israel "a Jew is a Jew is a Jew," as Gertrude Stein might have
said. There are even pious ones who study the details of
priestly sacrifice in anticipation of the rebuilding of the Temple and the reintroduction of the blood-and-incense rites recorded in the Torah. Others have less defined hopes and
merely take their election by God for granted. The first part
of the divine promise is apparently being fulfilled: the people cast forth to the four corners of the earth are being
gathered in. The land is once again a land resounding
with the holy tongue, children speak and sing it at play,
merchants and workers, housewives and government offi-

cials use it with the fluency—if not always the imagery or refinement—of the ancient Prophets. In the schools they read the Bible as their native classic. Its geography is history and present all at once. Meggido was a household word in antiquity; today an afternoon field trip from Haifa will make the old name live again in the minds of children. Beth She'arim was the burial place of ancient sages, and the sarcophagi are there to be seen. The mines of Solomon are once again in operation, and a restaurant on the shore of the Dead Sea calls itself Lot's Wife's Inn, for this is the area of Sodom and overhead loom rocky pillars which in the falling dusk glimmer with salty encrustations and tantalize you with their human likeness. Here as everywhere the Bible is alive, and the Bible is Jewish history and God's history too. It surrounds you, it speaks to you. Here above all the Covenant seems real.

And there is Jerusalem, there is Mount Zion. The Psalmist said: "Who shall ascend the mountain of the Lord and who shall stand in His holy place?"[4]—and here is the mountain beckoning you to ascend. The prophet dreamed of the day when men would call to each other: "Come let us go to the mountain of the Lord, to the House of the God of Jacob"[5]—you see the place, you walk its tortuous road up to its steeply cast summit, and if the House of God is not visible to you it is only because your sense of history is temporarily overcome by the mundane realities of a decadent present. It is not hard to be a believer in the city of David.

Yet all too many find it not only hard but impossible. Worse, they find it neither one nor the other. They treat the foundations of their faith with an airy indifference, which is breached only by annoyance over traffic restrictions on the Sabbath and by other less obtrusive manifestations of the past. Worse yet, there are Israelis who, though Jews by background or even upbringing, desire nothing more fervently than to be known as "Canaanites"—men living in the old land as natives, men without the encumbrances of Judaism, men without history, who like their Belgian cousin [of the previous chapter] want to be left alone.

The Canaanites are few in Israel, for so radical an approach is today palatable only to declared rebels, and besides, it takes a certain degree of self-knowledge to assume a philosophic stance. But there are more *de facto* Canaanites in Israel than is generally admitted. The land breeds them, for while in the Diaspora one has to do something with his Jewishness (or at the very least, one has to do something with his awareness of Jewishness), in Israel one needs to do nothing at all with it. The story is told of a little girl out in the country who with her blond tresses and pale blue eyes presents a textbook facsimile of the mythical Nordic Aryan. A tourist, much entranced by the girl's beauty, stops his car and asks her: "Are you Jewish?" The youngster is puzzled by the question. "No," she finally blurts out, "I live in the Kibbutz over there!"

One does not have to be a Jew in Israel, one can just be a person—so at least goes a popular saying, and many people are eager to live by it. They want to be like all the other nations of the world and they are prepared to work hard toward this goal. The socialist, anti-Orthodox and hence anti-religious tradition of the early immigration gives a strong impetus to this humanistic, leveling trend, and the rejection of God by so many former concentration camp victims does the rest. He forsook them in their hour of need, they say; now they will have no part of Him. The attempted abrogation of the Covenant is, if anything, more consciously pronounced in Israel than anywhere else. In the Diaspora the Jew walks away from God without knowing that he is walking away; in Israel the majority are well aware of the distance that separates them from the God of Israel. In the Diaspora the Jew would be uncomfortable if he had to face up to the reality of this separation; in Israel the Jew has learned to live with it.

This, in any case, is the outward appearance. There are those who say that the Jew in Israel has the same spiritual yearning as have men anywhere; that the surface diffidence is naught but spiritual bravado in reverse; that there as in the Diaspora neglect and rejection are passing phases of a distraught transitional age which has not as yet lived down the cruel memories of the Age of the Ovens.

CAN WE REJECT THE COVENANT?

Still, the possibility exists that neglect will become rejection, and that rejection is not love-in-hiding but real. The question then is, can Jews truly reject the Covenant, can they repudiate it in the face of an unrelenting God?

Individual Jews certainly can. It is possible to lay off the mantle of Jewish identity, or at least make the first motions to accomplish the end. What one Jew does not finish in his lifetime, his children may in theirs. Even the disingenuous Nazi *Sippenamt* (the Ministry of Genealogy) ceased its morbid gaze once it had satisfied itself that three grandparents of the suspect were unsullied Aryans. Given half a chance and ordinary circumstances a Jew can cease to be a Jew if he so desires. In fact, he always could. Formerly of course he had to convert to Christianity or Islam if he wanted to leave the house of Jacob. Today he need merely disassociate himself from the Jewish community, or change his name or intermarry and bring up his children outside the context of Jewish life. By adopting some or all of these contemporary devices his assimilatory designs will be met with success sooner or later. To be sure, there may be psychological problems on the way toward his oblivion as a Jew, and usually there are, but if a man is willing to pay the price he can forswear his allegiance to the Covenant. Apparently God is willing to let him go.

Whether the same is true for the Jewish people is another matter altogether. For it was the whole people who were the covenanting party, and individual obligation arose and arises out of the group's historical responsibility. And there simply can be no question of the Jewish people abandoning its history by a conscious act. Neither the instrumentality for such a disavowal exists, nor does the intent. Jews may be overwhelmingly indifferent to what God demands of them, but that is not the same as denying the demand outright. Men may disregard the law and even flout it on occasion without thereby giving assent to lawlessness itself. I do not even believe that today's Jews are really indifferent to the Covenant—and for this reason and based on this belief this book was first conceived. I think there is an ear to hear once there is a realization that God really has a Presence for man and especially for the Jew.

But suppose that the events of Ezra's day were to be repeated today, only in reverse.[6] Suppose the people were jointly to review their history and find that God had in truth forsaken them or that the original idea of being His servants no longer held any attraction for them? In ancient Israel they reaffirmed the Covenant; could they now choose to disavow it?

The question is, to be sure, theoretical and by its nature prevents any man from asserting that he could with any certainty know the answer. All of Jewish existence stands before the gate of uncertainty, for where the will of God is involved no man may say, "I know." Within the framework of this caution one may, however, attempt to speculate even about the unlikely.

The very impossibility of writing Jewish history in conventional terms, a subject with which we dealt earlier, appears predicated on a faithful God and a faithful people.

A faithless God would not be God, but is it conceivable that in the future the people may become totally faithless? The Prophets believed that Divine wrath was the consequence of faithlessness, although they did not contemplate an act of massive repudiation. They stated their case strongly; they exhorted their contemporaries with castigation, warning, epithets, and tears. At the same time they believed in a saving remnant, for there was a core around whom the future could be rebuilt. Was it for their sake, or for the sake of the thirty-six righteous ones that the book of life was never quite closed, that survival was the successor to destruction? At any rate, there was the remnant, and often there was a whole people who said "Yes" and thrice "Yes" to whatever God would ask of them. It was they who by their faith made the impossible an instrument of God's possibility. Had they too failed Him would there still be a Jewish people?

It is possible, although I do not believe it. Granted that God may need His people, there must be limits to His need in the full context of the vast universe. Certainly the biblical writer thought so when he pictured God as ready to set aside His love for Israel and start afresh. On more than one occasion Moses entreated Him to reserve or reverse the judgment. That the Covenant could end because of Israel's neglect, seemed then, and seems now, within the realm of the imaginable. A *formal* rejection of its heritage by Israel, akin to its formal acceptance of it, need not be considered. But *informal*, though no less expressive, rejection is a distinct possibility. In that direction we are well on the way.

Such rejection is composed of many individual acts and attitudes. By sheer accumulation it can become the people's spiritual stance. If enough Jews fail to take God seriously the condition is created whereby the faithful partner too will fail to sustain the historic situation. Ulti-

mately then, what needs to be done lies within the reach
of each Jew. One single man turning away may tip the
scales of existence; one single man turning toward the
sources of faith may uphold the Covenant for all. What this
may mean in the life of each will be the subject of the
following chapter.

JEW AND GENTILE

Meanwhile, we Jews are what we are. The attenuated
religious consciousness cannot hide the reality of our potential, nor can it obliterate the uniqueness of our position.
This in turn raises the question of our relationship to
Gentiles. If Jews continue to consider themselves as chosen,
how are they to view themselves in this egalitarian world?
And what are they to make of the other world religions
and especially of Christianity and its claims?

It is alleged that "Chosen People" is a dangerous concept, that it breeds or fosters the sin of racial superiority.
The allegation is in part true. The concept at issue is
volatile and can be harmful medicine if taken at the wrong
time or in excessive doses. A people oppressed will lash
back at the oppressor. If no other avenue exists it will
channel its ego defenses into self-adulation and contempt
for the enemy. This happened during the dark centuries of
ghettoization. The Jew was a third-class subject of the
king or state, but in the privacy of his home when he
welcomed the Sabbath Queen, in the comforting embrace
of the study house where he hurried after the day's work,
he knew that he was specially favored by Providence. Was
not the world steeped in illiteracy and ignorance? Did not
the humblest Jew have access to treasures which were
beyond the reach of worldly princes? What did the simplest
Jew, whose daily fare were discussions on philosophy and
ethics, have in common with the Russian *muzhik* or the

Arab *fellah?* Nothing except a basic humanity which all
too often seemed distorted and disfigured when viewed
through the prism of pogroms.

No objective student of history can deny that for nearly
two thousand years Jews were in fact, man for man, a people of superior education, of superior intellectual and spiritual training. What among other nations was reserved for
the few belonged to the lowliest laborer among the Jews.
A sense of superiority was inevitable under such circumstances; it arose from the realities of life more than from
preconceived theological notions.

But these notions reinforced and deepened the actuality
of difference. Jews were superior, so it appeared, not only
because of circumstances but because of innate disposition.
Jews were favored by the inheritance of Abraham and
Moses and, above all, by the choice of God. This, rather
than political and sociological configurations, could explain
their uniqueness. It explained at one and the same time
the reason for God's displeasure with His people—they had
sinned and were being punished in accordance with their
high spiritual station—and for God's favor to His people—
they were given an opportunity to prepare themselves and
the world for redemption.

Chosenness was thus part of the Jew's world outlook. But,
except for the darkest moments of his history, it did not
decay into contempt for others nor did it render him in-
sensitive to his own shortcomings. *Goy*, originally a word
for "nation" which applied to Jew and Gentile alike, became in time a pejorative with which the non-Jew was
designated. *Goy* was the alien, the uneducated; *goy* was
crudeness and bloodthirstiness; *goy* was the Cross or the
Crescent when it came with the sword rather than with
Bible or Koran. It was with these and their bloody execu-
tioners that Jews had contact, not with the genteel nobles
of a cultured princely court. Rabbis and priests had no con-

verse except at public debates where the object was not truth but conversion and where the wheel, the stake, and the fire were never out of sight. Chosenness was defense against the cruel and heedless *goy;* chosenness was the promise that made the unbearable bearable. If Jews want to cast it off today is it because they feel uncomfortable with these memories? They believe that their neighbors disapprove of such egocentric feelings and they hurry to disavow them as outmoded and superannuated.

In doing so the well-intentioned Jew confuses chosenness with superiority. The two ran hand in hand for so long that it is hard to separate them now. Chosenness can indeed be a paltry covering for spiritual emptiness and a pretense for unwarranted conceit. This danger exists, but it is worth risking. For choice can also mean the continued acceptance of the Covenant, the Yes to this unique relationship, this special set of obligations and opportunities. If it is to this that the Jew wants to say his No, then let him do so, but let him also know the real significance of his deed. God is at stake, not superiority, and the Jew cannot hide behind his professed dislike for the latter if he really wants to reject the Other One.

JEW AND PAGAN

From the earliest times the Jew was torn between two extremes when it came to the religion of other peoples. One was utter rejection and, if the opportunity arose, extirpation root and branch. The other was generous acceptance, the affirmation that the righteous Gentile too had access to salvation.

There is no point, at this late stage, to "defend" the Bible for its singleminded contempt of the Canaanites and their ways and for believing that co-existence of God and Moloch was impossible. The one demanded justice, mercy, purity; the other seemed to encourage a way of life in which human excess was given the halo of sanctity and in which human dignity counted for little. Where the two ways clashed in one land, one had to go, and this to the biblical Jew meant that its professors had to go as well. To the modern mind this is simply unacceptable and we count the Bible's demand for the extermination of the Canaanite nations a tragic misreading of God's will (the extermination never succeeded in any case, as the author of I Kings 9:21 regretfully notes). I do not believe that God wants us to kill unbelievers in order to smooth the way for His Kingdom. I hold with those biblical critics who believe that the early records of the nation, with its wars and incidents of violence, were later bathed in the post-factum light of presumed divine approval. The remarkable thing about these interpretations is that the Jews felt so strong a need to justify their wars when no one else gave it a thought since war was an accepted aspect of life which needed no defense.

The Bible leaves us in no doubt about the worthlessness of the pagan gods. They were useless at best, and abominable at worst. But when an Arnold Toynbee opines that this "Judaic" characteristic of religious exclusiveness was responsible for Christian and Moslem excesses, for their inquisitors and Almohadian fanatics, he is surely stretching a weak point. His argument deteriorates into a historical astigmatism of the worst sort when he makes the Jew ultimately responsible for the Nazis' megalomania.[7]

Jews insisted that Judaism was the best, the only religion for the Jew; and even though they dreamed at times of the day when "the mountain of the Lord's house shall be established as the top of the mountains,"[8] they did not insist that all the nations would have to become Jewish. Except for its own realm where God reigned alone and none could be tolerated beside Him, Judaism did not deny the right of other nations to worship as they pleased. It is no accident that the word *Elohim* describes the plural gods of the nations as well as the single God of Israel. "Let all the other nations walk each one in the name of its god, but we will walk in the name of the Lord our God for ever and ever," said the prophet.[9]

This is the second side of the coin of Israel's relation to other religions. The first is the rejection of paganism for oneself, the other its acceptance as a fact of life among the peoples of the world. To be sure, this acceptance had limits, for even of the non-Jew certain basic demands could be made. Jewish tradition enumerates seven so-called Noahide laws to which men might give assent through a proper understanding of natural law. The name derives from the covenant which God made with Noah and his descendants, in which He promised never again to destroy humanity because of its sins. In return, however, the sons of Noah, the B'nai Noah, as they were called, were given an opportunity to achieve the minimum standards of religion and morality set down for all men. What were these standards?

To be counted among the B'nai Noah one had to forswear idolatry, incest and adultery, bloodshed, blasphemy, robbery, legal and social injustice, and eating flesh cut from a living animal. If a stranger wanted to reside in Palestine he had to observe the seven laws.[10]

The acceptance of these basic principles earned a pagan the accolade of righteousness and the assurance of salvation. An oft-quoted dictum of the ancient sages sums it up: "The righteous of all nations have a share in the world-to-come"—the equivalent of eternal bliss. (Out of this concept Hugo Grotius, in the early seventeenth century, developed his theory of natural law which was the foundation of modern international law and a cornerstone in the development of the principles of equity.) To be a Jew was to be the possessor of a precious and unique heritage, and its observance his special task. Without him the world might never reach the goal set for man, but this did not mean that God wanted all men to be Jews. He could be served in other ways, and for this He had created the nations.[11]

JEW AND CHRISTIAN

But what of the Christian? What of the Roman and Greek Catholic with his statuary and his saints, with his adoration of the Mother of God, what of every Christian with Father, Son, and Holy Spirit—was he offending against the prohibition of idolatry? Did he therefore disqualify himself from being reckoned among the B'nai Noah?

To the Christian this question will probably come as a shock. He who for so long has decided who is and who is not to be saved, will he count the question as an instance of "Jewish arrogance" and unwarranted conceit? Before he commits himself to a quick emotional reaction, let him contemplate that in the middle of the twentieth century the great Roman Catholic Church in Council assembled was struggling with a declaration of religious liberty without yielding one iota of its cherished dogma that it alone has the truth. Let him contemplate that for near twenty centuries the Jew has found himself branded as steeped in stubborn error, buried in a dung heap of prejudice, unredeemed, and, as a Jew persisting in his folly, the unredeemable son of a deicide people. That the Jew in turn, as object of such Christian judgment, would deem the perpetrators of execrable cruelties, committed in the name of those whom they professed to adore, to be themselves the victims of idolatrous practices was natural and understandable, if not necessarily logical.

And Jews were not the only ones to view Christianity in this light. Moslems shared with Jews an overriding concern for keeping the oneness of God pure and unsullied. "Thou shalt not make unto thyself any graven images" kept both religions from exploring fully the arts of pictorial and sculptural representation. The Jew said *Sh'ma Yisrael,* "Hear O Israel, the Lord our God, the Lord is One," and made this phrase the nearest thing to a formal declaration of faith. The Moslem said *Allah il Allah* which meant the same: "The Lord alone is God." But Christians prayed to a triune God who was three-in-one; they lavished loving care on painting the man-god's pictures; they made icons and altars; they created statues and bent down before them. We should not be surprised if such practices struck Jews and Moslems as coming dangerously close to idolatry, to say the least. If Christians wanted to demonstrate the essential unity of the Old Testament heritage, they did their best to hide it behind an iron curtain of contempt for the mother religion. It was a tragic failure of spiritual communication, a failure which only now in the age of ecumenism, reconciliation, and dialogue is seen in all its disastrous extent.

Fate decreed that sooner or later Jews had to give a formal answer to the conundrum of their own problematic relationship with Christianity. During the mediaeval persecutions Jews were often forced to make the bitter choice between death and conversion. The traditional rule was that one should preserve one's life under extreme pressure even if one had to violate every law—every law, that is, except the prohibitions against idolatry, murder, and incest. When asked to commit any of these death was deemed the necessary choice. Could one therefore accept the Moslem or Christian faith without transgressing the law against idolatry? Here the issue was met, and the age's most revered scholar gave his unmistakable answer. Islam and Christianity, wrote Moses Maimonides, were not to be considered as *aboda zara,* as idolatrous worship. A Jew who became a Marrano, an apostate-by-force, would not forfeit his claim to the world-to-come. These religions were children of the mother who had brought them forth, and they too were instruments of God's will. Through them He was reaching toward a part of the Gentile world which for the time being was beyond the influence of Israel.[12]

This opinion was pragmatic but it also represented the special nature of Judaism which was both particularistic and universalistic in outlook. Jews had a task which no one else had; the nations of the world had their own responsibilities toward God and man. Jews and Gentiles ultimately belonged together, for the grand quest of humanity was theirs together. Each would go his own predestined way until the days of the Messiah would join them all at the throne of the One Universal Lord.

Alas, the recognition of Christianity and Islam as God-directed faiths was never given an opportunity to play a positive role in Jewish life. Oppression occluded the vision. How could a Jew in Europe believe that Christianity too had its roots in Providence if Christians debased the image of God in man so constantly, if they hated His children and tore each other apart in bloody wars and religious persecutions? Maimonides spoke theory; daily experience taught otherwise. So Jews would cringe when the very name of Jesus was mentioned, they would avoid pronouncing it and would circumscribe it with words, gestures, and epithets which expressed revulsion. They would turn away when passing a church. To them it was the place whence all their sorrowful debasement sprang. Christianity a servant of God? It was not a subject which Jews could discuss rationally. Jesus and the Apostles, the Church Fathers, and all the Christian piety of the centuries were outside the range of Jewish concern.

They were, but they cannot remain so. The slow but real repentance which all Christian churches are finally showing with regard to their "Jewish sin," has eased the climate sufficiently so that the Jew in turn may take another look at Christianity. For his own sake it is important that he do so.

The need to define the relationship weighs on him as heavily as it does on Christians.

Some of our people are still caught in the morass of yesterday's antagonisms. I am filled with shame when a contemporary rabbi argues whether it is permissible to recite the traditional memorial prayers in behalf of President Kennedy. The question was, the rabbi said, "whether Kennedy had a 'soul' in the Jewish sense." I have neither patience nor understanding for such dogmatic narrowness, which only beclouds the issue that must be faced.

I will not enter here into the presently fruitless discussion about "the Jewish Jesus and the Christian Christ." It is said that the former, as man and teacher, can be taken back into the synagogue and can be given a place in its history, while the latter, as Messiah and God, is the exclusive possession of Christianity. I will, however, speak clearly of how one Jew views the religion of his neighbors.

I take my stance with Maimonides and those who followed him and I draw the logical and inescapable conclusion: *If God willed Christianity, then surely it must be true that it is part of the ongoing process of divine revelation.* It has both failed and succeeded, even as Judaism has. Christianity attempts to speak to men in a special voice, and many men have heard through it the voice of the living God. They will continue to do so and I respect their quest and their genuine religious grasp. It is theirs, it is not mine. How much of Christianity has its origin in a direct apprehension of God I do not know, even as I do not know it with precision of Judaism.

Franz Rosenzweig, whose magic personality had an abiding influence on my religious development, once said that "God did not, after all, create religion; He created the world. And when He reveals Himself, that world not only persists all around us, but it is more created than ever. For revelation does not at all destroy true paganism, the paganism of creation; it only accords it the miracle of return and renewal. Revelation is always present. . . ." And he found it above all in what he called "the two distinct historical manifestations of revelation . . . Judaism and its antipodal offspring, Christianity."[13]

About this there can be no doubt: there is a special unbreakable relationship between the two faiths despite the love-hate tension that has characterized it for so long. The same Book, the same dreams for man springing from this Book, the same way of grasping the presence of divine opportunity—these and many more likenesses bind Judaism and Christianity in their long, agony-torn history. The Jew remains at the core, guarding the Eternal Flame, as it were, while the Christian goes into the world to speak in its own terms of Jewish hope. In this going out lies the constant danger of paganization, of diluting the Jew's keen sense for the oneness of all striving. Therefore, when a Christian loses his faith in a maze of conflicting claims, he often finds it possible to turn to Israel and its ways. The Chosen People forever holds its mystical attraction, for it offers to those within a unique means of serving God and man.

Beyond this, I look at Christians as partners in the struggle for a meaningful, God-filled tomorrow. I look at the varied manifestations of their faith with critical reverence. When the Council Fathers in Rome search their souls, I pray for them. Let them prepare their way toward salvation for those who choose to walk it. I rejoice in the breadth of Christian piety and the depth of its commitment even as I am saddened by the exclusive view it still exhibits of itself and of the world around it. And I know only too well that in my own realm of responsibility there is so much to do. My own people have stumbled and their eyes are dimmed. To them above all I must speak words of comfort and of warning. The "cobwebs of exile," as Rav Kuk called them, still hang on our brows even when we dwell in Israel.

JEWISH MISSIONS

The election of Israel does not preclude the election of others. I neither judge other claims nor do I denigrate them. God works in many ways. All those who are part of Israel and its Torah are thereby partners to one particular fateful choice. This choice is open to all, and as David Polish put it, "all who pledge themselves to Torah qualify."[14] Should it not then be our task to bring others into this special relationship, to make this unique opportunity for service available to all who might desire it?

The enormity of the Jew's own inner problem of faith and identity seems to obviate all need to contemplate Jewish missions to the outside world. But does it? Has the Eternal People not demonstrated the most varied resources in dealing with the complex demands of its existence? Can it not do one more task, especially if such a task may in the very doing revitalize the people's divine enthusiasm?

Let no one think little of this argument. If Jews today could be convinced that what they have to offer is urgently desired and liberally welcomed by millions of people, Judaism would take on a new hue of promise for the Jew himself. Sometimes it does take others to make one appreciate one's own possessions. It is true for spiritual, artistic, and intellectual values as well as for material things.

Four questions arise:

Does this inner nature of Judaism permit of missions and converts?
If so, what kind of mission could be contemplated?
Would the world be receptive?
Could Jews be convinced and mobilized for such a program?

From the earliest times the Jewish people have grown physically and often spiritually by accretion from the outside. The Moabite Ruth became the ancestress of King David and his Messianic house; Onkelos, the authoritative Aramaic translator of the Torah, was a convert, and so were many others throughout antiquity. Paul of Tarsus remarked admiringly of the Pharisees that they were wont to go to the ends of the earth in search of souls. Colonies of old and new Jews could be found from the reaches of the Ganges to the Rock of Gibraltar.[15]

The monolithic organization of the Christian and Moslem states changed all that. Apostasy from the Gentile community was deemed a criminal offense, the consequences of which were visited on the Jewish community that dared to accept such a defector. In self-protection the Jewish outlook first on missions and then on individual conversions changed radically. Converts became a communal danger, hence they were undesirable. If would-be converts applied nonetheless, innumerable obstacles were placed in their way; they were rejected several times to test their sincerity; it was made clear that to be saved they need not become circumcised practicing Jews, they could assure their spiritual future by observing the rules laid down for the B'nai Noah. In consequence, all missions ceased and, except for the mass conversion of the Khazars in eighth-century southern Russia, proselytes became exceedingly rare.[16] In time this was taken to signify a permanent development in Jewish-Gentile relations. Jews were welcome to accept the religion of their hosts, but the reverse did not hold true. In fact, it simply ceased to have significance.

This is the continuing attitude of the so-called traditional wing of contemporary Jewry. They want no converts, and the fewer applicants the better. It is an attitude commanded by sentiment, not by reason. It lays stress on descent rather than conviction, on folk rather than faith. It is in some respects quasi-racial in nature. I cannot share this attitude and I do not think that Jews should, in justice both to themselves and to those who seek admittance.

Of course, Jews can never approach the world and say: Join us for we alone have the truth and through us alone is Eternity assured. To say so would run counter to all we believe. I do not for one moment contemplate detaching a single soul from a faith that fills and satisfies his life. But I do consider it desirable to say to millions of people who flounder on the seas of doubt and searching: Here is a people whose sane and humane practices, whose social idealism and strong loyalties can set a steady course to your aimless drifting. Here is a faith and a Covenant which we are glad to share with all who would make it their own. You will have to learn the heartbeat of this ancient folk and you will have to resolve that in joining it you will also become a partner to all the vicissitudes that may lie ahead, as well as to its fulfillments and its glories. The door is open, it is up to you to pass it by or to enter. I would say no more and no less, and most important, I think it ought to be said loudly and clearly in Europe and America, in inner Africa and in Japan.

For I believe the time is now. The spiritual vacuum in the world is widening. The traditional missionary religions may have reached their zenith. The world is hungry, and not for bread alone. Perhaps I read the Book of Man wrongly and deceive myself, for here too the wish may be father to the thought. The constant stream of converts now being accepted, primarily by liberal rabbis, is a faint but sure indication of our potential. The growing interest of Gentiles in all cultural and religious offerings of the synagogue is another. I believe that millions are waiting at the gates, waiting for a word of encouragement to make their first hesitant entry.

But the Jews, I fear, are not ready to open. They are

timorous, steeped in old habits and old prejudices about the racial characteristics of those not born into the fold of Abraham. They worry about the possible inimical reaction of the nations in whose midst they dwell—a groundless but nonetheless strong anxiety. They are above all unsure of their own meaning and future. Here lies the chief reason why missions to the Gentiles, desirable and timely and even necessary though they are, will not be carried on by any of the major groups in Jewish life. They are not clear about their relationship to the Covenant and the God of the Covenant. How then can they draw others into the sacred circle?[17]

I have a dream, a dream of a people turning its scarred yet youthful face toward the shining light of Sinai and stretching out its hands toward both the heights of purpose and the nations of this world. We are few today, very few. The army of the Lord should welcome recruits for the task whose meaning is shrouded in uncertainty.

A PEOPLE DWELLING ALONE

Meanwhile we dwell as we have always dwelt, alone.

> Lo, it is a people that shall dwell alone,
> And shall not be reckoned among the nations.[18]

It has been thus since Balaam's time, in war and in peace. No political alliance ever touched the inner nature of Israel and Judah, and no spiritual alliance ever wound its cords about the soul of our people. Apartness was the price of uniqueness, and what at first seemed spiritual necessity—to separate the people from its pagan environment—became in time the single most significant aspect of its existence.

The very parlance of the Western world reflects this. "East and West" is a perfectly understandable division of geopolitical equals. "Intellectual and non-intellectual," "white and dark races," "Christians and non-Christians," "believers and unbelievers"—all these distinctions are obvious in their corelation and balance. But "Jew and Gentile" takes up the ancient prophecy of Balaam and perpetuates a contrast which numerically is preposterous and culturally without apparent content. Yet there it is: Jews use it as do others, as if the world could be so divided, between a small, scattered, battered folk who form an infinitesimal portion of mankind, and all the others! It makes no sense, unless of course one views the improbable *sub specie aeternitatis*. We Jews are a people dwelling apart, we are not reckoned among the nations.

We fostered and encouraged the idea by our religious and social habits. We could not eat the non-Jew's food nor drink his wine. We lived together for outer and inner security. The ghetto walls forced us to do what in many ways we might have done voluntarily. Now that they are gone we still huddle together in the warmth of our fellowship, the protective sentiment of past and present, and in the face of real or imagined rejection by the world around us.

We remember how we dwelt alone in concentration camps and rode alone in cattle cars and died alone in nameless, shapeless forms. We clung to each other—to whom else might we have clung? We cried, but who heard us? Even when the full horror of Auschwitz was known and we begged the leaders of the West to bomb the railroad yards of that infamous charnel house where ten thousand men, women and children were being unloaded every day of the year, the planes "could not be spared" as the politely regretful reply was phrased. Death came, as it always comes, to each one alone—six million times alone.

The Negro's plight today has at last become the white man's agony of conscience. It is good that this is so; it is late, and we hope, not too late. The Negro too has dwelt apart, but color and history are subject to attenuation and change, and change is the script of tomorrow. In time, his apartness will diminish because the Negro, though apart, will not be alone. But the Jew will be what he was. For his anchor point is the awesome, hidden Other One who Himself dwells alone. Aloneness is the existential burden of the Jew. He is, as tradition and meaning convey, *kadosh,* holy and separate at once.

Speak to the men who represent the State of Israel around the world, in the capitals of the Gentiles. No one speaks her tongue. No other nation is deeply and passionately concerned about her existence. Whether she lives or dies may touch the diplomatic chords of the harp of peace, but the instrument would play a dirge as quickly as it would a dance. Israel has allies *de convenance;* it has no friends unto death. She belongs to the West but dwells in Asia, while most of her citizens stem from Africa and Eastern Europe. Her neighbors deny her the right to live and the world accepts such attitudes as if they were the normal fare of international relationships. There is an aura of unreality about it all, fit for a play if the actors were not so real and the implications not so gruesome. Her neighbors cry "Death to Israel!" and they mean "Death to every Jew!" The nations of the world think of power ploys and balances. They did it then, in the days of Hitler, and they do it today. Meanwhile, the Chosen of the Lord dwell alone in the rock-filled Land of Promise and "are not reckoned among the nations."

For better or for worse, Jewish existence has this quality. Tradition speaks of the "yoke of the Kingdom of Heaven," knowing that to be involved with Heaven is a burden as well as a joy. A midrash connects Sinai with the word *sin'ah,* hatred.[19] Perhaps the latter is always directed against the covenanters of the former. Separateness is the yoke of the Jew. It demands a heavy price; it demands it of all and of each. It tears the soul with longing for the embracing friendship of the nations, and it drives us back to the lonely post of waiting. It aims its beam into the heart of every Jew, searing some and illuminating others. Our psyche is burned by desire and rejection, by forgetting and remembering, by openness and withdrawal.

It is worse today than it has been for many years. In the midst of affluence and physical security, we are adrift and know not why. We are alone and know not why. For we have lost touch with the true center of our existence, which gives meaning to what we are and which turns the yoke about our neck into a shining collar of glory.

CHAPTER VI

The Demands of Faith

To be a Jew in the twentieth century
Is to be offered a gift. . . .
The whole and fertile spirit as guarantee
For every human freedom suffering to be free,
Daring to live for the impossible.

Muriel Rukeyser
"Letter to the Front"

If the people, as a people, dwells alone in time and space, what can we say of the individual Jew? Is he not a man among men, a friend amid friends, a citizen dwelling with and in his society? He is; yet in the deepest context of his existence he too is alone.

I speak here not of Jewish sociology in the Diaspora. Much has been written on this subject: on the basic failure of the individual Jew to become an integral part of his environment; on the "five o'clock shadow" which appears after working hours and falls across the social and personal relations between Jew and Gentile; on the exclusion practiced by social clubs and top business echelons which successfully prevents the Jew from entering the power structure of the community. All these exist for the time being in larger or smaller measure wherever Jews dwell in dispersion. They do not exist in Israel, of course, at least not for Jews *qua* Jews (although there is sociological "aloneness" for certain subgroups in the country). The sense of being alone to which I refer here is cosmic in nature. It has to do with man's place in the universe, his losing and finding anchorage, his rootedness in the Ground of Being, as Tillich would phrase it. And for the Jew it has to with the Covenant: what it says not merely to the people, but what it continues to say to the single one in the midst of the people.

For the *b'rith* involves not only the many as an amorphous historical mass. If it has meaning it can achieve such meaning only in the lives of those who call themselves Jews. Each one is addressed and each one must hear it on the level of his existence. He may be unresponsive, he may turn away, he may even pretend not to hear and not to be addressed at all—or he may "listen and do" as his fathers did. The great Why of Jewish history consists of millions of small Whys across the ages and lands: "I make this covenant . . . not with you alone, but . . . with those who are not with us here this day."[1]

I was addressed then and I am addressed now. On my decision may hang the fate of God's people and, perchance, that of the whole world.

On my decision? To say this may seem utter presumptuousness, the arrogant conceit of which Jews have so often been accused. Does not the lofty disregard of the nations for this infinitesimal people hold up such pretenses to well-deserved ridicule? But I make the claim of individual significance not for myself alone, not even for my people alone. I make it for every man, in all times and circumstances. "Significance" is an arbitrary human term weighted with relative meaning. What may appear centrally important to even the most discerning human eye may in the course of events become marginal. We speak of "trends" and "social conditions" that shape human history, but whose action or thought turned a potential trend into a rel-

evant factor? The unknown and unknowable ingredient
consists of the omissions and commissions of single ones in
the uncountable swirl of human kind. An old rabbinic adage
says: "One man is equal to all the works of creation," and
another: "He who sustains one life, it is reckoned unto him
as if he had sustained the whole world."[2] This thought not
only enlarges the meaning of the good deed itself, it also
points to the ineluctable possibility that the one life sustained *was* equivalent to the whole world. The tale of the
thirty-six righteous ones who maintain justice and make suffering bearable (I have referred to this in Chapter iv) here
assumes another dimension. For it is an essential aspect of
the legend that none of the thirty-six knows that he is so
chosen. Potentially, then, every man may be a secret saint,
a *lamed-vavnik*.

THE REMNANT

The Prophets long ago spoke of the remnant who would
keep the Covenant alive and reconstitute the people.

A remnant shall return, even the remnant of Jacob,
Unto God the Mighty.[3]

Our less prophetic age knows of the *sh'erith ha-pletah*,
the remnant of the European destruction, which is not really what the Prophets had in mind (they foresaw the cy-
cle of guilt and salvation because of evil and righteousness,
respectively, and never dreamt of punishment without sin).
Yet one can speak of a remnant in the midst of a physically
secure Diaspora or even Israel, a remnant of the spiritually
disintegrating people, a remnant who take the Covenant
seriously. Rabbis know them as the faithful few who pray
and study, who set righteousness above all else and who
know that there is One who makes demands. They understand the oft-repeated story of the Hasidic rabbi who one

day sent out an urgent call to all the people in the town
to assemble at once at the market place. The artisans left
their benches, the shopkeepers their stalls, the women came
with their children. When they were all together the rabbi
addressed them. "I have a most important message for
you," he said with the holy intensity for which he was famous. "Your very lives depend on it." The mass of faces
before him were turned expectantly and reverently toward
the master. "This is the message," he fairly shouted: "There
is a God in the world!"

A God in the world? The people looked at each other in
dismay. This was no news to them, they were all believers.
Was it for this that they had interrupted their working day,
merely to hear a sermonic fragment of dubious depth, a
truism?

"There is a God in the world!" the holy man repeated.
Slowly the words penetrated. The crowd fell silent, each
one preoccupied with what the rabbi's reminder meant in
his own life. For if there is a God in the world and one
becomes aware of Him in the hurly-burly of the every day,
then suddenly one is face to face with the devastating,
shattering question: What does He want of *me?* How will
I know His will, and how will I know that it is His, not
mine?

I come here to a question that has puzzled men ever since
they glimpsed that other Reality. If there were a clear-cut
answer I would not need to write of it: it would be self-
evident. The prophets could say: "Thus saith the Lord,"
and say it with an inner assurance which burst forth from
their souls even when they resisted the message:

> The Lord God hath spoken;
> Who can but prophesy?[4]

How did they know? That they had a special spiritual sensitivity seems beyond doubt. With most of us moderns this

sensitivity has atrophied; we have developed other capacities and developed them well. Some day perhaps we may again learn how to listen to the still, small voice and "know" another's heart as a man "knows" his wife. The evolution of man may well be, in its next stage, an evolution of spiritual powers which men once possessed to some degree and which they may again acquire and strengthen beyond our present imagination.

THE SLOW ASCENT TO FAITH

Meanwhile the noise and the tumult that press on us shut out what even now we might apprehend. Only occasionally can we manage to open the shutters: in prayer, in solitude, or wherever we suddenly are exposed to "knowing" in the deepest sense. How can I convey it except by restating what in essence cannot be stated at all, for the Ineffable defies definition, the moment of speaking and hearing is gone almost before it begins. But in the aftermath I know, with a knowledge grounded in my humanity, in being what I am. I may know no new facts and have no certainty; I only see a path, a direction, a must. Reflection clarifies it without changing its essence. It is no leap of faith, far from it. It is a slow ascent, but faith it is and it speaks to me and my condition and out of me and as I am.

I am a Jew. You who will read these words will be Jew or Christian, Buddhist or Moslem, or you will perchance —the chance is large!—wonder what you are. Being is a kind of total apprehension; thought, emotion, background, learning, fears, and hopes—all these are part of it, yet their sum is less than being. So it is with knowing that there is a God; so it is with knowing that life is worth living, that truth, love, mercy, and justice are real and that in respect to them something is demanded of me. I have not always known this; the knowledge is *sui generis* and not always available to me. It seems to acquire a crust which hardens with every day of spiritual neglect. Let it harden long enough, and the task of breaking it becomes painful and often frighteningly so. I listen to those who speak to me of their deepest anxieties: this fear of opening up to admit the God who demands is as great as any they experience. There is after all a "fear of the Lord," all our self-assured poise cannot deny it. We do fear the confrontation with ultimates, as a consequence of which we might have to change and change radically. It is as simple and as complex as that.

I am a Jew, and I listen as a Jew. I can do little else. I cannot listen as a "man" any more than I can listen as an "average man." I cannot listen as a Christian. Had I been raised in a different environment I would be listening differently. Neither can I listen as a Hasid, nor will his hearing be like mine. We are individuals, totally unique each one of us, and we can only hear what we are capable of hearing. Tradition has formed our ears, so to speak.

I hear God in the context of my tradition. If it seems necessary to affirm it once again, let me repeat: Everyone can be so addressed. Spiritual capacity is a universal human endowment; it is no more confined to Jews than it is to Christians. Each man speaks out of what he is. "Here I stand, I can do nought else," Luther said. I think I know what he meant, from his stance.

And just as he, a devout Christian, was shaped by his tradition and yet felt driven to go beyond it, so may a Jew be driven and in conscience be bound to hew out his own path. For man is free, every man, and Jews are no exception.

But they too start somewhere. They begin with the Covenant and with tradition. What they do with these will form them. Out of these they hear and act. Without lie many worlds of thought and feeling, within lies Judaism.

If you say that I have closed my ear to other voices it

may be true. I have not consciously closed it; still, it cannot be helped. I am like one who wants to hear music and finds that to do so he must go to a concert. When he wants to hear a speaker he must go to the lecture. When I want to apprehend the demands of Israel's God I must go to the living waters of Jewish tradition. I know of no other way.

THE WAY OF TARYAG

Tradition speaks of 613 commandments that are obligation and opportunity for the Jew. Since in mediaeval Hebrew numerals were expressed with letters, *taryag* represents the number 613, and anyone familiar with the significant aspects of Jewish life would know that *taryag mitzvot* answered the query: What must I do to fulfill God's law? If I observe these, or at least observe them as carefully as I can (since no man can expect to do God's will completely), I have opened the door to His antechamber. The 365 negative and 248 positive commandments are the Jewish way of serving God. This is the teaching of Orthodoxy.

No part of life is left out of the range of these laws. From morning till nightfall and after we are under their sacred sway. There are times for prayer and there are fixed prayers to fill these niches of time. There are phylacteries to put on head and arm, and the how as well as the when of wearing them are meticulously prescribed. At certain occasions one must be wrapped in a prayer shawl; at all occasions one must wear a garment bearing special fringes; and at no time may one wear *sha'atnes*, cloth made of a mixture of faunal wool and floral flax.

There is food one may eat, and there is the whole Gentile cuisine which is forbidden. There are wines which are allowed, and others one may not swallow. There are days for fasting and days when fasting is against the law.

There are holy days and week days, and all have their

religious format. The child is born and males are circumcised on the eighth day; some boys must be redeemed on the thirtieth day from the ancient obligation of Temple service; all must study and learn, marry and propagate. Few of the positive ritual commandments which depend on a special time for observance are incumbent upon the women. For not only were they accounted inferior religiously (no pious reinterpretation can set aside this historical fact), but they were supposed to be busy with mundane though necessary daily chores like raising children and earning a living. But the negative commands apply to them too: women too must observe the Sabbath and refrain from transgressing upon its sanctity; they must guard the home against all defilement, and they are left in no doubt how this is to be accomplished.

There is living and there is dying. All is part of *taryag mitzvot*, for the one who dies and for the one who stands at the grave and spends prescribed days in prescribed ways of mourning and remembering.

There is the synagogue with its demands, and the house of study with those pertaining to it. There is the market place of life and the sanctuary of the home. It is in the home above all that God's presence is made visible. Traditional Judaism is at its core a home-sanctifying way of life, though it by no means denigrates the house of God or demeans the vital importance of ethics and moral behavior in all spheres of existence.

Quite the contrary. The home is merely the natural center which molds one's character and reinforces one's desire to serve God in all ways. Hence there are *mitzvot* for conduct toward our fellow men; they are strict and demanding. They know nothing of convenience but much of sacrifice and rigorous ethical codes. God is exalted by deeds of loving kindness and by acts of justice toward our neighbors; He is diminished when we injure His image in His children.

And there are blessings for every act we undertake, for every moment which comes into the purview of consciousness. We eat, and we praise Him for His bounty. We see a great man, and we praise God for the privilege. We are saved from danger, and thank Him; we bring our son to the Torah for Bar Mitzvah, and thank God for allowing us to pass this step in our religious responsibility. We perform the natural functions of the body, and thank Him for health; we hear of death, and praise Him as the righteous judge. All of life is a constant opportunity for divine service. God is always within reach.

If all of this makes it appear as if traditional Judaism is a vast and intricate network of ritual do's and don'ts which must be observed for their own sake, this is inevitable. Here lies its strength and its weakness. For while the goal is the creation of a more perfect man, the way leads through the little deeds. One does not build character merely by desiring it; there must be habituation, and this is achieved through *taryag mitzvot*. In addition there are also the special duties devolving on us simply because we are Jews: no one else needs to be circumcised; no one else needs to eat certain foods and abstain from others; no one else needs to observe the Sabbath in our way—for ours is the Jewish way, our own particular path toward salvation.

THE DANGER OF EXTERNALIZATION

What if the exercise of *mitzvot* becomes routine? What if the ancient problem of externalization is thereby aggravated? This was the charge against the Pharisees, and since it was much overstated it led to a totally false image of Pharisaism. For while it was true that Pharisaic Judaism stressed the meticulous adherence to the Law as the rabbis had developed it, it was simply not true and purely polemical to say that this was their final goal.[5] They warned insistently against mechanical and pedantic performance. The traditional Judaism of today which developed from their labors uses the observance of particular acts as the means to elevate man into a constant state of divine readiness. *Mitzvot* are to achieve the pious life. They always point beyond themselves. Only human weakness confuses the means with the end.

But the danger of externalization does exist. We are human and are prone to spiritual satiety.

Even the pious ones are not exempt. They tell the story of the Hasidic sage who often delayed his morning prayers because he had to spend considerable time to ready himself for worship. "I pray that I may be able to pray," he said. Meticulousness will tend to become pedantry; habit all too often overcomes spontaneity.

A contemporary example will illustrate the problem as the Orthodox Jew sees and meets it. He is forbidden to write or answer the telephone on the Sabbath, because these actions constitute labors proscribed for this day. There is one exception, however: in the exercise of healing and saving life one may, in fact must, disregard the Sabbath rules. Consequently a nurse serving in a hospital may attend to her charts and use the telephone. But a *responsum* by Chief Rabbi Isaac Unterman of Israel provides that a nurse who must violate the Sabbath in this way should do so in a manner which would constantly remind her that she does it only for the sacred purpose of sustaining the life of her patients. How? If she is normally right-handed let her write with her left hand on the Sabbath; if she ordinarily takes the telephone in her left hand let her reverse it in the exercise of duty on the Sabbath. In this way she will remember that what she does is an exception and may not become the rule. It was inevitable that some time after this decision was issued a nurse who had carried it out faithfully reported that she had become ambidextrous. What next? It is obvious that every rule will draw another in its train.

This is an unavoidable danger, inherent in the system of *taryag mitzvot.* Most of the commandments are specific rules rather than general guidelines. And whenever the law is specific it must take pains to cover as many exigencies as possible. Since Jewish law means to encompass all of life it must be applicable to any and all circumstances. This calls for immensely ramified rules and highly detailed prescriptions, and these in turn have to be subdivided into ever smaller capillaries so that the life blood of divine service may reach every tissue of existence. Where the law fails, there will be the precedent of thousands of years and the ready counsel of rabbis trained to see that God is served with heart as well as with hand.

If the Jew stumbles in the process to achieve the highest rungs of service, at least he knows that he is on the right road. Like many another person at worship he too may say his prayers while preoccupied with the extraneous thought that he must hurry to meet some mundane demand, but at least he says them, and he knows that somewhere, somehow he has been reminded of the divine presence. Tomorrow perchance he will be able to pray truly. He may attend services only because his friend's son is called as a Bar Mitzvah and he feels an obligation to his friend rather than to God. Still, says an old proverb, though he comes with muddied motives he may learn to come thereafter for the pure sake of coming.[6] The ways of God are obscure and so are the sure ways of serving Him.

But if certainty is lacking, security is not. The Orthodox Jew knows that he is always on the way, for in the last resort the *taryag mitzvot* are of God. He is their author and He has set these laws for His people to do, but not to question or alter.

Here is the hub of Jewish tradition. Its implications are clear: everything reflects the will of God, from the laws of Sinai to the minutest detail of ritual regulation today. In a sense everything was revealed already to Moses, if not explicitly then implicitly. The Torah, Israel's constitution, contains the seed for all future growth, and the rabbis of succeeding generations merely explain the law in answer to new questions. They do not develop the law, which is immutable: "You shall not add anything . . . or take anything away from it."[7] Rabbinic law is therefore an aspect of divine will. This is why the blessing over the Sabbath candles speaks of God commanding the act although the Torah merely demands that we observe and sanctify the day, without specifying precisely how it is to be done. It is on this level alone that the prayer which women recite on the eve of the Sabbath has meaning: "Blessed art Thou, O Lord our God, King of the Universe, who hast sanctified us by His *mitzvot* and has commanded us to kindle the Sabbath lights."

The function of the rabbis throughout the ages has often been compared to that of Anglo-Saxon courts, and specifically to that of the United States Supreme Court when it interprets the American Constitution. But such a comparison is inaccurate. Anglo-Saxon legal tradition sees the courts as *developing the law* rather than as attempting to state its original meaning. "Due process" today is not necessarily what the Founding Fathers intended it to be. The court does not pretend that its present use of the concept reflects that of Jefferson; rather, it frankly imposes its own contemporary understanding on the old phrase.

In Europe jurisprudence is in this respect much closer to the Orthodox Jewish idea. There, the constitution is not considered so elastic as to admit of broad development. If

new times demand new laws then let the law be changed,
but let it not be corrupted and bent into unrecognizable
shape. The constitution is considered more rigid by French-
men than it is by Americans.

A case in point was a dispute before the United Nations
in the fall of 1964. At issue was the failure of the USSR
and potentially of France to pay special peace keeping
assessments leveled by the UN. The General Assembly and
the International Court had held that these assessments
were obligatory under the United Nations Charter. The
Americans agreed, the Russians and French disagreed. The
latter (aside from obtruding political considerations) were
on firm ground from their point of viewing the United Nations Constitution, and the United States could refer with
equal strength to its legal tradition as supporting the opposite. It was, among other matters, a clash of legal traditions.

Jewish Orthodoxy would, I think, understand the French
way of approaching the problem. It maintains that what is
asked of the Jew today essentially was asked of his fathers
at Sinai. Circumstances differed of course, but then as now
it was God and not man who gave the law and sustained
it.

An old midrash illustrates this approach. When Moses
is on Mount Sinai he asks God to show him what will become of his precious Torah. God complies with his wish
and miraculously transports him forward in time to the second century of the Christian era. He sets Moses down in
an academy among students who listen to a lecture by the
renowned Rabbi Akiba. The sage is expounding a knotty
legal problem and gives his decision in the matter. Alas,
Moses understands little or nothing. His perplexity in-
creases when a pupil asks Akiba whence he derives the
authority for his answer. "Because," he is told by the
teacher, "this was already revealed to Moses at Sinai."
Whereupon Moses, pleased at the compliment though in-

tellectually in great confusion, asks God to bring him back to his own time and circumstance.[8]

What the author of this midrash meant to convey is apparently this: You may wonder how much of what we do is really related to Sinai and Torah and God. But you should know that the connection exists and is strong. It was God then and it is God now who made and makes His demands on you. These are the old demands revealed to Moses; there is nothing novel about them. The rabbis only make clear what is needed today to understand the ancient revelation.

The Roman Catholic Church approaches its own tradition in identical fashion. Its councils and popes "uncover" the truth, they do not create it anew. *Aggiornamento* is the updating of externals, it does not concern essentials. The Vatican Council cannot "develop" the Gospels. It will always claim that its pronouncements uncover the *original* meaning of the Scriptures, a meaning which was always there but had been overlooked or misunderstood through the ages. This is essentially the traditional rabbinic way. God's law is static, revealed and stated once and for all.

This is the way of *taryag mitzvot*, but it can no longer be mine, nor can it be walked by any who do not accept the literal divinity of the biblical text.

THE STRUGGLE OF THE LIBERALS

Once I depart from the premise of the sustained divinity of Jewish law I am faced with the need for creating a new rationale for Jewish living. Is there any authority for observance or is it all the way of free choice? If it is the latter, how is the choice to be made? And how does the Covenant, how does God relate to the choice? The number of these questions and the obvious problem of answering them satisfactorily makes it apparent that if you can accept traditional theology you will have an easier time of it. It is in many ways easier to be an Orthodox than to be a liberal Jew—and I suspect this holds true for Christians as well as for science and politics. The Orthodox know their authority and their duty. The liberals struggle to know both, and meanwhile they are not excused from acting on partial or tentative knowledge.

Where do I turn for authority? I am not speaking here of the complex question of the source of moral authority and of autonomy in the Kantian sense. To do so lies outside the range of this book. But having said this, I have of course not done away with the problem. If God ultimately determines the nature of what I ought to choose, then how free am I altogether? If God needs me, as I believe He does, is my need not divinely circumscribed and its fulfillment determined? I will state my approach without attempting to justify it philosophically. (It ought to be stated that liberals should not be the only ones to ask these questions. They are, however, among Jews anyway, usually the ones who do and have done so in modern times.)

My answer must of course start with the Covenant. I see in it an obligatory relationship between God and myself—not myself as a detached person, rather myself as a Jew, a member of the people. My obligations flow from a triple relationship: between God and the people, between the people and me, and between God and me. As a Jew I relate to God only in the ways of my people, else I am not a Jew in the deepest sense of the word.

My answer is further conditioned by a fundamental commitment to the proposition that man's distinguishing trait is his freedom to make existential decisions. This means that I as an individual—and I am here concerned with the individual—can exercise my choice only out of what I am: by heritage, by obligation to my people, my parents, my children, to society. And since some of these factors are variable, and since I myself am changing, my decision will not, nay need not, always remain the same.

Take as an example the question of philanthropic largesse that constantly exercises the Jewish community. How much may be expected of an individual? Are there objective standards, which relate a man's financial status to his moral responsibility? Let us assume that the needs of the people are objectively assessable. May the individual claim that it is his and not someone else's understanding of these needs which represents the true measure of his responsibility, if any?

Now there are some who by upbringing and character find it so painful to give to any degree that they are incapable of making a decent contribution to the common weal. I once knew a very rich man who told me with disarming frankness: "Please don't ask me for more. I cannot bear to do it; it hurts too much." I have never been able to despise this man; he needed education and help, not contempt. I sincerely believe that given his personality and state of moral growth, he probably could actually not do more. It may well be that in the conflicting demands made on him he acted within the limits of his freedom. This does not excuse the man's social failure. I could not bring myself to be his friend and neither could many others. He was an incompletely developed person, a grasping infant in adult guise.

It is apparent that at the lower end of the scale—where understanding is lacking altogether because of physiological or psychological insufficiency—there can be no responsibility at all because there is no freedom. The law which exempts the insane from criminal responsibility would agree. As a general rule society will attempt to protect itself from social undesirables, if by no other means than isolation or ostracism. It is one thing to understand a man's limitations;

it is another to pretend that therefore no objective obligation exists at all.[9]

At the upper end of the scale are men whose sense of duty is such that they reach beyond their capacity. In wartime society dispenses medals to these persons; in philanthropy they may gain the accolades of their fellow men and in any case obtain the satisfaction which come from fulfilling the *mitzvah* of giving. They too are free; only their freedom is large, and therefore also their duty.

Therefore, I will begin where I must, with the uncertain possibilities of my freedom. There is consequently a fundamental difference between the traditional way and mine. The former is fixed; there are 613 clearly defined guideposts to salvation. In the liberal view the guideposts move; they may become partially invisible or disappear while new ones may come into view. And I who seek the way, I myself see differently at times, more clearly now, less clearly perhaps tomorrow. Often I will go by memories of yesterday, by the memories of my people, by its records of memory, from Bible on until today. I may do less today and more tomorrow. Quantity is not decisive, quality is. The how and why, the devotion, or *kavvana*, the inward turn to God—these count above all. I change and so does my ability to choose, to hear, to listen. And listen I must—this is demanded of me.

What then shall I hear? That which I am capable of hearing out of my own individual existence, and that which I hear through the collective historic voice of my people. I must search not merely for *my* God but also for the God of my people. The prayer book speaks of "our God and God of our fathers, God of Abraham, God of Isaac, God of Jacob." Why the threefold specification? Because God is both the God of my people and at the same time the God of the patriarchs individually. Each of them had to find Him in his own personal way. Similarly I too must search

and find my God out of the dual condition of my self and
my people. I too must aim to say: "My God and God of
my fathers." In the unique relationship between Him and
me the listening of my people plays its momentous role.

THE IGNORANT CANNOT BE PIOUS

I must know how my people have understood the demands of the living God, how they have struggled, have
sometimes failed, sometimes succeeded. I must know its
sancta and its folkways, its concept of *mitzvah* and the way
of *taryag*. Without such understanding I am cut off from
the moorings of the Covenant. Ignorance cannot be a
foundation for Jewish religious living. In this sense the old
adage applies: "The ignorant cannot be pious."[10] Jewish
education is therefore an objective obligation for the people
of the Covenant. It extends to children and adults; there
is no upper age limit to learning, no degree which once
achieved excuses the bearer from further study. Extent and
intensity of the learning and reading process are conditioned by the Jew's individual capacity; the need for the
mitzvah itself is not.

And upon the foundation of knowledge I must build my
own house of life. In meditation and prayer I must reflect
on what I—the specific, unique I—can do to fulfill my part
of the Covenant. Here is my listening: concerned with God
and people, and with my own ability to understand and
act. Not slavish preservation of the past is at stake, but
what Buber called, "the ceaseless begetting and giving
birth to the same single spirit, and its continuous integra-
tion into life."[11]

It is less important, therefore, what I do than why and
how I do it. It is important that I make decisions about
my spiritual life. Drifting is akin to sinning, it marks con-

tempt for my potential and obligation. At the beginning
stands concern.

Israel is my concern and among the *mitzvot* I undertake
must be some which contribute to its survival. Rescue work
and philanthropy belong in this category, as do Jewish
education and Jewish marriage. The peoplehood of Israel
is my concern. To it I owe a sense of self-assumed discipline. Some will choose abstinence from certain foods or go
beyond it to the maintenance of special restrictions. They
will decide to abide by folk practice, not because of their
intrinsic merit, but because "this is what the people do." It
is an ancient guideline already found in the days of the
Talmud.[12] The way in which I observe holy days, festive
occasions, and days of mourning should reflect my identification with the continuing peoplehood of Israel.

Man is my concern. The moral and ethical demands
upon which my tradition has cast its radiant beacon belong
at the heart of my existence. "Thou shalt" and "Thou shalt
not" may or may not be direct commands from God, but
they are part of my relationship with Him, a relationship
illumined by the spiritual struggle of my fathers.

God is my concern as I am His: this is the core of the
Covenant. I approach Him alone, yet even alone I am part
of the Covenant people. My son is circumcised for God's
sake (to sanctify his body) and for Israel's sake (to sanctify
the covenant with Abraham). It is my *mitzvah*. I fast on
Yom Kippur for God's sake and for Israel's. I eat the *matzah*
on Passover for man's sake (a remembrance of my obligation to the cause of freedom) and for Israel's sake (a remembrance of yesterday's struggles and today's needs). The
bread of affliction becomes my *mitzvah*. Judaism's message,
Buber once said, is that man must begin. *I must begin.* Then
the deed is born and on the bridge of deeds, truly per-
formed, the Jew meets his God.

THE DEED, THE MITZVAH

Concern alone is not enough. There must be deed, some actualization of intent. Contemplation must ripen into will, and will must flower into action. But which? Here lies the dilemma of the liberal. His understanding of the command makes him a variable in the equation, for he comes to the decision with his background, his emotions, his upbringing; and further he may understand one thing today and another tomorrow. He may do much or little, he alone will determine it out of his being, his listening, his relation to Covenant and people.

I have respect for the Jew who on the basis of meditative decision eschews most of the ritual law, even as I respect him whose option is for maximal observance. I have the deepest respect for the decision of a Franz Rosenzweig who, coming from an assimilated environment and at one time ready to embrace Christianity, found his way back to the Covenant and accepted for himself the discipline of Orthodox tradition. He remained a liberal—this was his life's stance, though to all appearances he was a staunch traditionalist. On the other end of personal decision stand men like Samuel Holdheim a hundred years ago in Germany and Emil G. Hirsch a half century ago in America. They were men of the highest moral drive and deepest social conviction, true believers, messianists in their way, and they had the ability to open to their contemporaries their own glorious vistas of high purpose. Holdheim, for instance, was willing to give up circumcision and the Saturday Sabbath. To Hirsch who became the progenitor of many of Chicago's welfare institutions the forms of religious life meant little; he considered them outdated or superstitious. For many years his temple did not even have the most basic of all Jewish worship accouterments, a Torah scroll.

He reintroduced it toward the end of his life, an example of willed and purposive change.[13]

Holdheim and Hirsch represent the extreme development of the Covenant to its formless idealization. I respect their point of view as a genuine expression of their religious stance. I also believe that their position would have been more palatable if they had been in less commanding positions of leadership. As it was, they opened the door to those who only saw the abjuration of ritual and were not prepared to follow the leaders' active concern for man. The result was a widespread rejection of all traditional *mitzvot* and the utterly mistaken notion that "being Reform means doing less." Nothing could be further from the proper meaning of liberalism.

Historically speaking I consider the Holdheim-Hirsch interpretation of the demand made on the Jew as a dead end of nineteenth-century optimism. It was nearly deaf to the voice of the Covenant people. It individualized the Covenant to a degree where it became a relationship only between God and the single one, with the Jewish people fading indistinctly into the wings of history. But in effect this meant the erosion of the Covenant itself and therefore tended toward the de-Judaization of life. In time the radical liberals, like Hirsch himself, turned back toward their people. Before they did so, however, they had caused many to follow the path of a covenantless, vague—if often enthusiastic—humanitarianism.

THE CALL FOR DECISION

In so criticizing this trend I do it from the only vantage point I know: my own. I concede the same right, that is, to evaluate positively or negatively my reading of demand and Covenant, to liberals of all shades as well as to the Orthodox. *Jewish life need be no more uniform than life on*

any social, cultural or religious level. Uniformity of outlook
and practice are to me neither desirable nor possible. They
never did exist in Jewish life, though it is true the spread
of diversity we see today is unprecedented. The Covenant
asks for sincerity and decision, not for conformity.

But I repeat: it asks for decision. It cannot be satisfied
with indolence, neither in doing nor in not doing. Doing
"more" is in itself no indication of spiritual maturity. I can
accept the traditional dictum that there is no difference
between "big" and "small" *mitzvot,* since only God knows
their full impact on the world. I cannot accept the conclusion that therefore one must do them all, since they are
all of equal weight. They are not; if they are so to others,
they are not so to me. "Big" and "small" are terms that
need to filter through any will and understanding.

So I examine my life in the light of my tradition and
in the knowledge that what I do must have meaning in the
triple relationship of God, Israel, and myself. And I who
make the decision am both what I am and what I can be.
My reach must exceed my grasp. It is not enough for me
to do the reasonable, the comfortable, the accustomed.
Forever I must ask: "Is it enough?" If I follow tradition,
I must ask this question, and I must posit it when I am
prepared to reject it. I cannot reject lightly; this above all
I cannot do lest I end by contemning the Covenant. Like
everyone else I construct my totem pole of values, and
prayerfully I reorder them from time to time, subtracting
some, adding others. As I grow older I seem to add more
often. It happens invariably at the end of a reflective period
in my life, when I am more open to the Other One and
to the cry of my fellow man. Then the Covenant speaks
more urgently to me in the way Franz Rosenzweig must
have experienced it, as a "divine incursion."

For in search of answer, said Emil Fackenheim, "the
liberal Jew of today must encounter the ancient reflection

of the divine incursion which constituted the covenant under which he still stands. He must also encounter the
tradition of those of his ancestors who sought—and received
—answers before him. But if and when he himself receives
an answer as a result of this encounter, it will be—if the
encounter itself is genuine—the answer heard by him with
modern ears, and addressed to him in a modern situation.
Heard by him it will no doubt bear the stamp of his human
interpretation, just as did the answers heard by earlier generations. But if it is a genuine answer, genuinely heard,
his human interpretation will nevertheless be the result of
God's address. For He, the God of Israel, still lives; and
the liberal Jew, son of the Covenant, still stands at Mt.
Sinai, as did his fathers."[14]

LIVING IN TWO WORLDS AT ONCE

The liberal, like the Orthodox, faces a basic religious
dilemma. He too stands in constant danger of routinizing
what was at first a fervent decision. Practice makes for
habituation, and habituation dulls the edge of will. You will
say that this is all to the good when the practice is good.
True. The man who has learned to give or to pray should
be encouraged in the constant actualization of his religious
motives. But he must also know that there is no limit to
either deed or will. The possibility of deepening our concern must never be stunted. The uncertainty of the Covenant finds its parallel in the shifting uncertainties of one's
own potential. What I can do and what I can know will
never be enough. In every way the liberal lives an open-
ended existence. What he does is only his partial answer
to the demand, and what he knows bears necessarily the
stamp of incompleteness. He must learn to live with partial
answers, with "holy insecurity" as Buber put it, and he
must learn never to take the part for the whole. This is

what renders his task so demanding: to live with but a glimpse of ultimate truth.[15]

Upon the Jew in the lands of dispersion this task falls with added weight. For to inner tension he joins the problem of living in two worlds at once: that of the nation to which he belongs as a citizen, and that of the Jewish community to which he is bound across time and space. The Jew who wills to live in *golah* (i.e., in separation from the Holy Land) thereby chooses to live in a culture which he aims to transcend by his own spiritual nature, yet at the same time one to which he owes allegiance and concern. Far from impeding him in the exercise of this duty, his religion encourages him to take it most seriously. This has been true since the days of Jeremiah, who wrote to the Jews in Babylon, "Seek ye the peace of the city . . . and pray unto the Lord for it; for in the peace thereof shall ye have peace."[16] Jews have made an almost desperate effort to become part of the environment and to enrich it whenever they were given any chance at all of identifying themselves with it. Only when they were continually repulsed, as in the ghetto days of central and Eastern Europe during the last few centuries, did they draw completely into their self-protective shell and leave the world at large to others. Parochialism is not an innate part of Jewish living, as the relatively brief experience of Jews in western lands has amply demonstrated. Where they have been able to throw off the shackles of past anxieties and have gained confidence in the reality of freedom, they have sought the "peace of the city" with all their might.

They have entered every avenue of public and private expression, from the arts to politics, from writing to entertaining. They have become culture creators and culture consumers. They have—most important of all—sought new social frontiers.

They have been rebels and fighters, radical at times, reticent at other times. Not all have heeded the call to social justice; there are still many to whom any cause without the adjective "Jewish" has little or no appeal. In this the Jews may be, as Heinrich Heine put it, "like other people, only more so." But Jews cannot be satisfied with this, for the Covenant under which they stand speaks of justice, not Jewish justice, of righteousness without adjectival fetters, of love unrestricted and knowledge unlimited. God was and is the God of Israel and He was and is the father of all men. The Jew is a parochial being in that like everyone else he faces himself first of all, and he is emphatically a universal being, facing the world and its burning tasks. The Jew in *golah* makes the needs of the nation in whose midst he dwells his own, even as that nation has made him its own. His civic loyalties belong to it; his human loyalties belong to all men; his spiritual loyalties belong as always to the God of the Covenant.

What of the Jewish people to whom physically and spiritually he is welded with bonds of history? Can there be conflicts in these multiple loyalties?

The answer must obviously be yes. All life is a resolution of conflicts, for this is what every decision represents. We owe multiple loyalties within our own family, within the basic quadrate of husband-wife-parent-child. We stand in the vortex of concentric communities, cities, states or provinces and country, of professional, fraternal and a host of other relationships which make a legitimate claim on our loyalties. We each have our value scale and make our choices accordingly. We vote out of a complex of preferences, some narrow and others wider, and our natural progression rises from the core of the self to the periphery of universal concerns. This is the way of man, and rare are they who can reverse the order. Yet when the reversal does occur in the form of sacrifice and principled rebellion against the conforming tides of human pressures, the conflict is cast into bold relief: suddenly we know that the usual value order will not do, that there are higher goals and higher purposes which demand preferred adherence. "My country right or wrong" has no basis in morality; "My country, may she always be right" has the ring of realism mixed with skepticism and hope.

It is sometimes said that the existence of Israel as a political community poses the threat of dual loyalties for Jews in Dispersion. I think this is true only in a limited sense. Israel as a state, as a distinct national, legal entity has no claim upon the Jewish citizens of any land. But the Jewish community in Israel, as a unique core group of the Eternal People, does have such a claim. It has to do with our joint task in the Covenant, and as such is of transnational and transnatural character. It is akin to claims which the Christian citizen of any country experiences with respect to the Church Universal; they too transcend the national loyalty he otherwise accepts completely.

The Jewish argument is muddied because Israel is often called the "Jewish State." However, the state is not truly Jewish unless the facts bear out its theocratic nature. It is a secular state whose citizens confess various religions or no religion at all and who are equal partners owing every allegiance to the polity but possibly none to its presumed Jewishness. There are Israeli Jews and Israeli Moslems, Israeli Bahais and Israeli Christians. The Jews are in the majority and it is this and the fact that it is the Land of Promise which make the state unique in the context of Jewish life. The Jewish community in Israel, not the State of Israel as such, has a claim on me. The two may enjoy a large measure of congruence, but that does not make them identical. This is not merely a fine distinction; it is of the essence.

Here as elsewhere the Jew is caught in the cross fire of history. He lives in two worlds at once and is subject to the tensions of both. He is dominated by the past, yet free to strike out in new directions. He is challenged to decide for himself, yet limited by his capacity to decide unequivocally. He searches for his fathers' God, and must find his own. In the midst even of his own people, he like the people stands alone.

CHAPTER VII

Personal Postscript

Home is where one starts from. As we grow older
The world becomes stranger, the pattern more complicated
Of dead and living. Not the intense moment
Isolated, with no before and after,
But a lifetime burning in every moment
And not the lifetime of one man only
But of old stones that cannot be deciphered.

T. S. Eliot
"East Coker"

Throughout this book I have spoken of "God"—as if the use of the word itself excused me from explaining its meaning. I have put it off because to speak of it necessitates that one become autobiographical, to some extent, for in the end I can only speak of *my* God and the God of *my* people. The two are inseparable. Thence the increasing frequency of the personal pronoun in the later chapters and hence these brief notations on the writer's own "uncertain mission."

Thinking, speaking, and writing on the nature of God and of revelation—in other words, on matters theological—was surely furthest from my mind when I was a young man, and it did not become urgent for me to do so even during the earlier years of my rabbinical career.

I grew up in Germany, in Berlin, where my parents directed an orphanage. Both parents came from Orthodox families, my father from an old Hessian family in the back-

woods of the Schwalm, and my mother from a Rhenish-
Westphalian background. But in Berlin they had turned
to liberalism. My father had a deep appreciation for history; biographies were his favorite approach to a knowledge
of the past. His intellectual curiosity was great and his library appropriately extensive. We were surrounded by
books as well as by the special sounds that came from the
throats of a hundred children of varying ages. On the third
floor of the institution was a two-hundred-seat synagogue
which my father put at the disposal of a liberal congregation he had helped to found. We were brought up in a
Jewish atmosphere which was an integral part of our lives.
The holy days were sacred occasions for which the whole
house prepared. Even if I had had no calendar I would
have known the arrival of Sabbaths and festivals: without
fail my blue serge suit appeared, freshly brushed, a visible
reminder of the rhythm of the year. We went to services
as a matter of course. There was never any discussion about
it, or if there was I have forgotten it. We were Jews and
the Jews I knew attended worship services regularly. It was
a matter of natural procedure and not a matter for argument.

But none of us, neither my younger brother (he too became a rabbi) nor I nor my parents were contemplative by
nature. We were activists, we liked to *do* things. We were
encouraged to think, but as my father was wont to quote,
"not the thought but the deed is of the essence." Our religion was a natural acceptance of our heritage, it had the
tinge of German liberalism, it was rational, without the
trappings of emotional fervor. It tended to be outward looking and later assumed political overtones.

Learning came easily to me. I read a great deal, especially on history ancient and modern, and in my later years
of adolescence my father and I engaged in mnemotechnical
games which centered around names, dates, and other often

NOTES

Chapter I

1. The stories are related in Genesis chs. 12 and 20. For a historical evaluation of these events see *The Anchor Bible, Vol. 1,* tr. with an introduction and notes by E. A. Speiser (New York: Doubleday, 1964), pp. 91 ff. Speiser explains that Abraham's behavior was easily understandable in terms of ancient Hurrian custom. But the biblical narrator no longer recalled this and therefore Abraham's "recourse to half-truth, if not outright deception, was just so much anachronism." In other words, there was really no need to picture Abraham in this light.

For a homiletical interpretation, see W. Gunther Plaut, "Thou Art My Sister," *Central Conference of American Rabbis Journal,* April 1962, pp. 26 ff.

2. "The Manager," in *Certain People of the Book* (New York: Knopf, 1955), pp. 130 ff. The Isaac story is found in Genesis ch. 21 ff.

3. Gen. 49:6. [Biblical citations are to the translations of The Jewish Publication Society of America, Philadelphia.]

4. *Histories* V 2.

5. Exodus Rabba 5:13 and 14.

6. Amos 3:8.

7. Babylonian Talmud, Gittin 56b.

8. Bab. Talmud, Gittin 55b–56a.

9. *Histories* V 4. But later (V 9) he forgets this fable and says that the Holy of Holies contained nothing.

10. Cf. Joseph John Williams, *Hebrewisms of West Africa* (New York: Dial Press, 1930).

11. Cf. especially Malcolm Hay, *The Foot of Pride—The Pressure of Christendom on the People of Israel for 1900 Years* (Boston: Beacon Press, 1950); Jules Isaac, *The Teaching of Contempt: The Christian Roots of Anti-Semitism,* tr. Helen Weaver (New York: Holt, 1964).

12. Origen (4th century) is generally credited with having given impetus to these Christian attitudes when he said that "the Jews . . . nailed Christ to the cross" (*De Principiis* IV 8). Chrysostom is

quoted by Hay, *op. cit.*, pp. 27 f., and Bernard, p. 55. Although Bernard held these views he served as a restraining influence on crusaders whose anti-Jewish excesses caused untold suffering.

13. John L. Stoddard's *Lectures,* 10 vols. (Boston: Balch Bros. Co., 1897), II, p. 213.

14. Cf. William L. Shirer, *The Rise and Fall of the Third Reich* (New York: Simon & Schuster, 1960); Raul Hilberg, *The Destruction of the European Jews* (Chicago: Quadrangle Books, 1961).

15. *Op. cit.*, p. 195. Stoddard visited Palestine in 1874.

16. *Shulhan Arukh* means literally "Prepared Table," for it is meant to contain Israel's spiritual nourishment readied for everyday use. Caro composed his compendium during the middle of the sixteenth century.

17. Reubeni (16th century) was a Jewish adventurer who claimed to have been born in Arabia and who promised military conquest of Palestine; Sabbatai (17th century) was a Turkish Jew who managed to arouse fervent Messianic hopes among his people. Two good biographical novels have recaptured their lives, dreams, and disappointments: Max Brod, *Reubeni, Prince of the Jews,* tr. Hannah Waller (New York: Knopf, 1928), and Josef Kastein, *The Messiah of Ismir, Sabbatai Zevi,* tr. Huntley Paterson (New York: Viking, 1931).

18. *Op. cit.*, II, p. 220.

19. Hess wrote *Rome and Jerusalem,* and Pinsker, *Auto-Emancipation.* Both books were published during the second half of the nineteenth century.

20. The name was bestowed on Jacob after he had wrestled with the angel: Gen. 32:29.

Chapter II

1. Ezra 34:30; Isa. 65:23; Isa. 5:7; Exod. 19:6.

2. See the discussion in Maimonides, *Guide for the Perplexed,* tr. M. Friedländer (several editions), II, Ch. 29; Bab. Talmud Pesahim. 54a. A more recent translation of Maimonides is Shlomo Pines's *The Guide of the Perplexed,* University of Chicago Press, 1963.

3. A collection of references is found in Louis Ginzberg, *The Legends of the Jews,* Vol. VI, (Philadelphia: Jewish Publication Society, 1928), p. 30, n. 181; p. 39, n. 214; p. 32, n. 185.

4. See W. Gunther Plaut, *The Rise of Reform Judaism* (New York: Union of American Hebrew Congregations, 1963), p. 140.

5. See below, p. 170.

6. "Judaism in the Church," *Hebrew Union College Annual*, Vol. II, (1925), pp. 125 ff.

7. Matt. 27:25.

8. Koran 45:15; 3:73. Abu Mohammed Ali, also called Ibn Hazm al-Zāhiri, is quoted by Hartwig Hirschfeld, "Mohammedan Criticism of the Bible," *Jewish Quarterly Review*, Vol. XIII (1901), pp. 233 f.

9. Koran 6:47; 5:85. The quotation from Moslem tradition is taken from Samuel Rosenblatt, "Jews and Islam," *Jewish Social Studies*, Vol. II (1942), p. 73. For further information see *Encyclopaedie des Islam*, s.u. Yahud.

10. Quoted by J. Bergmann, *Jüdische Apologetik im Neutestamentlichen Zeitalter* (Berlin, 1908), p. 145.

11. Bull of July 5, 1247. Aquinas' view is stated in his *Summa theologica* II–II, 10:8: *Infidiles . . . nullo modo sunt ad fidem compellendi.*

12. Quoted by Martin Stöhr, "Martin Luther und die Juden," in *Christen und Juden*, eds. Wolf-Dieter Marsch and Karl Thieme (Mainz-Göttingen, 1961), p. 132.

13. Quoted by Jacques Courvoisier, "Calvin und die Juden," *ibid.*, pp. 141 ff.

14. Quoted by H. J. Barkenings, "Die Stimme der Anderen," *ibid.*, p. 228.

15. Quoted by Rudolf Pfisterer, "Sein Blut komme über uns," *ibid.*, p. 33.

16. Quoted by R. R. Geis, "Judenmission," *Allgemeine Wochenzeitung* (Düsseldorf), March 6, 1964, p. 19.

17. Michael Schmaus, "Das Verhältnis der Christen und Juden in katholischer Sicht," *Judaica* Vol. V, No. 3 (Zurich, 1949), p. 189.

18. Charles Peguy, quoted by Karl Thieme, *Judenfeindschaft* (Frankfurt am Main: Fischer Verlag, 1963), p. 7.

19. The principles were called "Schwalbacher Thesen"; *ibid.*, p. 74. On Pius' statement see Paul Demann, "Kirche und Israel in ökumenischer Sicht," in *Christen und Juden*, p. 279.

20. *Kirchliche Dogmatik*, IV 3, Pt. 2 (Zollikon, 1960), p. 1007; and especially his address, "Die Judenfrage und ihre christliche Beantwortung," *Judaica*, Vol. VI, No. 1 (1950), pp. 67 ff., where he asks: "Is the Old Testament right after all? Is it true that there is a faithfulness in which God eternally turns to men?" (p. 68).

21. "The Relation of Christians and Jews in Western Civilization," *Central Conference of American Rabbis Journal*, April 1958, pp. 18 ff.

Paul Tillich calls Judaism the corrective against paganism that lives within Christianity.

22. The book was published in Romanian, under a title meaning "Judaism Unmasked." Since the volume proved greatly embarrassing to the Soviet hierarchy it was quickly withdrawn and the editor publicly labeled as a benighted ignoramus. On Lenin's point of view see Abraham G. Duker, Introduction to Ber Borochov, *Nationalism and the Class Struggle: A Marxian Approach to the Jewish Problem,* selected writings, ed. Moshe Cohen (New York: Young Poale Zion Alliance of America, 1937), p. 20. See also Karl Marx, *Zur Judenfrage* (1st publ. 1844), *A World Without Jews,* tr. and ed. Dagobert D. Runes (New York: Wisdom Library, 1959), and Karl Kautsky, *Foundations of Christianity,* tr. Henry F. Mins (New York: S. A. Russell, 1953), pp. 150 ff.

On the Jewish socialist movement and on Socialist Zionism, see below, p. 69.

23. *Der Untergang des Abendlandes* (Munich, 1922–23), Vol. II, p. 247. Further quotations are from pp. 249, 393, 399, and 635. Spengler deals of course with many historical forces of which the Jew is but one.

24. Published by Alfred Knopf, New York, 1956. For professional critiques of Toynbee see Pieter Geyl, *Debates with Historians* (New York: Philosophical Library, 1956); Herbert J. Muller, *The Uses of the Past* (Oxford University Press, 1952); Pitirim A. Sorokin, "Toynbee's Philosophy of History," in *The Pattern of the Past* by Pieter Geyl, Arnold J. Toynbee, and Pitirim A. Sorokin (Boston: Beacon Press, 1949).

25. Arnold J. Toynbee, *A Study of History,* 12 vols. (Oxford University Press, 1934–61), V, pp. 658 f. Further quotations are from VI, p. 63, and VIII, p. 290, footnote. On the Chosen People, see XII, pp. 541–42.

26. Translated by Katherine Jones (New York: Knopf, and London: Hogarth, 1939). The two quotations which follow are found on pp. 212 and 215 (Eng. ed.).

27. *Mystery on the Mountain* (New York: Harper, 1959), p. XII.

28. *Ibid.,* p. 139, quoting John Bright.

29. The literature on the men and movements briefly alluded to in the text is very large. For an analysis of the various writings one may consult Meyer Waxman, *A History of Jewish Literature from the Close of the Bible to Our Own Days,* Vol. IV (New York: Bloch, 1941), and Jacob B. Agus, *The Meaning of Jewish History* (New

York: Abelard-Schuman, 1963), especially Vol. II. Among Christians who subscribe to the "survival" theory, James Parkes and Robert H. Pfeiffer may be mentioned prominently.

30. This is the title of a book by Mordecai M. Kaplan (New York: Reconstructionist Press, 1958), founder of the Reconstructionist movement. See also his *Meaning of God in Modern Jewish Religion* (New York: Behrman, 1937), and Eugene Kohn, *Religious Humanism—a Jewish Interpretation* (New York: Reconstructionist Press, 1964).

31. It should be noted that Ahad Ha-Am proceeded from the conviction that Jews had a superior ethic, by virtue of an innate ability to see moral values.

Chapter III

1. Job 13:15.
2. Deut. 29:13–14.
3. Ps. 81:5.
4. Cf. Deut. 30:11.
5. *Amid These Storms* (New York: Scribner, 1932), p. 293.
6. For a survey of contemporary opinions see Speiser, *Genesis* (The Anchor Bible, Vol. 1), pp. xx ff.
7. Letter to Martin Buber, 1925, *Briefe* (Berlin, 1935), p. 535. A similar view was held by the Hasidic teacher Mendel of Rymanov. He suggested that Israel at Sinai heard only the letter Aleph, i.e., the first letter of the opening word of the Decalogue (see G. Scholem, in *Commentary*, November 1964, p. 39). According to Maimonides, Israel heard only inarticulate words which Moses had to interpret (*Guide for the Perplexed*, II, ch. 33).
8. The passage discussed is I Sam. 15. Buber's brief essay is found in *Commentary*, January 1962, p. 63.
9. "Everything is in the hand of Heaven except the fear of Heaven," Bab. Talmud, Berakhot 33b.
10. The biblical reference is to Exod. 24:7. For midrashic references see Ginzberg, *Legends of the Jews*, Vol. VI, p. 30, n. 181.
11. Mekhilta Bahodesh 3, 65a; Bab. Talmud, Shabbat 88a.

Chapter IV

1. Isa. 53:3 and 52:13.
2. Isa. 42:1, 6–8.

3. Isa. 53:11.

4. *Kiddush ha-shem* means "sanctification of God's name" and represents the act of witnessing to His holiness at any cost. The term came to be identified with martyrdom for the sake of God and Torah. Parents would kill their children and themselves lest they fall into the hands of either the Church or its more earthy persecutors. Often such martyrdom was faced with great confidence: "They went joyfully and with singing to their death as if they were going to a wedding," an admiring priestly reporter wrote about the pogroms of 1349. A Dominican friar recorded: "Joyfully they hurried to their death as if they were dancing. First they threw their children and then themselves into the flames so that they would not, yielding to human weakness, do anything against their religion." Quoted in *Christen und Juden*, p. 113.

5. The tradition goes back to Talmudic days. The figure thirty-six is derived from the verse "Happy are all they that wait for Him" (Isa. 30:18). The Hebrew word *lo* (for Him) has the numerical value of thirty-six, for each letter of the Hebrew alphabet doubles as a numeral. See Bab. Talmud, Sanhedrin 97b, Suk. 45a. A memorable novel on this theme was written by André Schwarz-Bart, *The Last of the Just*, tr. Stephen Becker (New York: Atheneum, 1960).

6. Quoted in Plaut, *The Rise of Reform Judaism*, p. 138.

7. Exod. 10:26.

8. *Dieses Volk* (Frankfurt am Main: Europäische Verlagsanstalt, 1955), Vol. I, p. 131. [An English translation by Albert H. Friendlander was published in 1964 by Holt, Rinehart & Winston, Inc., and the Jewish Publication Society under the title *This People Israel*.]

9. Charles and Dorothea Singer, "The Jewish Factor in Medieval Thought," *The Legacy of Israel* (Oxford University Press, 1927), p. 182.

10. See M. Güdemann, *Jüdisches im Christenthum des Reformations-Zeitalters* (Vienna, 1870).

11. *Polemische deutsche Schriften* (Erlangen, 1841), Vol. 3, p. 46.

12. Louis I. Newman, *Jewish Influence on Christian Reform Movements* (New York: Columbia University Press, 1927), p. 617.

13. Rabaud St. Etienne, the Protestant pastor who pleaded for his own group and its quest for equality, also made a strong appeal for Jewish rights. See Simon Dubnow, *Weltgeschichte des jüdischen Volkes* (Berlin, 1928), Vol. 8, pp. 86 ff. See also M. Grégoire, *Motion en faveur des Juifs* (Paris, 1789).

14. Exod. 19:23. Many scholars consider untouchability and taboo originally to be constituents of the concept of holiness. Consequently that which makes holy also makes unclean (see *Universal Jewish Encyclopedia*, Vol. 9, *subj.* Purity, Ritual). That which is *kadosh* must therefore not be touched by strangers for they will breach its separateness. Cf. Joel 4:17.

15. *Judaica*, Vol. VI, No. 1 (1950), p. 69.

16. *Ibid.*, p. 71.

Chapter V

1. M. M. Kaplan, *The Future of the American Jew* (New York: Macmillan, 1948), pp. 211 ff. See also Reik, *Mystery on the Mountain*, p. 148.

2. By Thomas B. Morgan in *Look*, May 5, 1964, pp. 42 ff.

3. Charles Angoff, *National Jewish Monthly*, November 1964, pp. 10 ff.

4. Ps. 24:3.

5. Isa. 2:3.

6. See Nehemiah, chs. 8 and following.

7. Toynbee, *A Study of History*, XII, pp. 541–42. Marxism too is called a child of doctrinaire "Judaic" teaching.

8. Isa. 2:2.

9. Mic. 4:5.

10. Bab. Talmud Sanh. 56a–60a; Maimonides, *Yad*, Hilkhot Melakhim 9 and 10; other passages mention thirty laws to be observed, Jerusalem Talmud, Aboda Zara 2:1. The most comprehensive study of this subject is by P. Biberfeld, *Das Noachidische Urrecht* (Frankfurt am Main, 1937).

11. Bab. Talmud Sanhedrin 105a. See also Nathan Isaacs, "The Influence of Judaism on Western Law," in *The Legacy of Israel*, eds. Bevan and Singer, pp. 383 ff.

12. In his *Yad*, Maimonides discusses when it is obligatory to die for God and Torah (Hilkhot Yesode Ha-Torah V). On the relationship of Judaism to Christianity and Islam see Kaufmann Kohler, *Jewish Theology* (New York: Macmillan, 1918), pp. 427 ff.

13. *Franz Rosenzweig: His Life and Thought*, ed. N. N. Glatzer (New York: Schocken, 1953), pp. 101–2. Rosenzweig considered Judaism and Christianity as the only religions not specifically "founded" —in contradistinction, for instance, to Islam, which was created as a religion from the very start.

14. *The Eternal Dissent* (New York: Abelard-Schumann, 1961), p. 111.

15. On this subject see the comprehensive study by Bernard J. Bamberger, *Proselytism in the Talmudic Era* (Cincinnati: Hebrew Union College, 1939).

16. See the article "Chazars" in *The Jewish Encyclopedia*, Vol. IV, pp. 1 ff. Some scholars believe the conversion to have taken place a hundred years earlier.

17. For some years The Jewish Information Society (with headquarters in Chicago) has worked in this field. Since it has been inadequately supported its effect has been limited. In Jerusalem too a small group is engaged in attracting and converting Gentiles.

18. Num. 23:9.

19. Bab. Talmud, Shabbat 89b.

Chapter VI

1. Deut. 29:13–14.

2. Aboth de R. Nathan, ch. 31.

3. Isa. 10:21. "A remnant shall return," Hebrew *she'ar yashub*. In Jer. 11:23 the remnant is called *she'erit*.

4. Amos 3:8.

5. There are a number of competent scholarly studies on Pharisaism. See, e.g., George Foot Moore, *Judaism in the First Centuries of the Christian Era* (Harvard University Press, 1927), Louis Finkelstein, *The Pharisees* (Philadelphia: Jewish Publication Society, 1962), and the studies by Travers Herford and Leo Baeck.

6. Jer. Talmud, Haggiah I 5.

7. Deut. 4:2.

8. Bab. Talmud, Menahot 29b.

9. A contemporary discussion of this problem may be found in Erich Fromm, *The Heart of Man* (New York: Harper, 1964). His conclusion is presented on p. 143.

10. Ethics of the Fathers II 5.

11. *Israel and the World* (New York: Schocken, 1948), p. 143.

12. Abbayye's dictum is found in Bab. Talmud, Erubin 14b.

13. On Holdheim, see Plaut, *The Rise of Reform Judaism*, p. 122 and *passim*. See Emil G. Hirsch, *My Religion*, (New York: Macmillan, 1925).

14. *Commentary*, October 1960, pp. 301 ff.

15. See *Martin Buber: Writings*, ed. Will Herberg (New York:

Meridian Books, 1956), pp. 20 ff. F. A. Doppelt and D. Polish in *A Guide for Reform Jews* (New York: Bloch, 1957), p. 41, take a similar approach for their definition of *mitzvah*.

16. Jer. 29:7.

Chapter VII

1. *Mein Weg als Deutscher und Jude* (Berlin, 1921), pp. 122 f.
2. Cf. W. Gunther Plaut, *Judaism and the Scientific Spirit* (New York: Union of American Hebrew Congregations, 1961), p. 5.
3. Leo Baeck, *Das Wesen des Judentums* (5th ed., Frankfurt am Main, 1922), p. 114. [*The Essence of Judaism*, a rendition by Irving Howe based on a translation from the German by Victor Gruben-wieser and Leonard Pearl, was published by Schocken in New York, 1948.]
4. *Ibid.*, p. 124.
5. See Glatzer, *Franz Rosenzweig* . . . , pp. 284 f.
6. Quoted in Zvi Kolitz, *The Tiger Beneath the Skin* (New York: Creative Age, 1947), pp. 94 f. Hayim Greenberg, the late publicist (1889–1953), held that unless one could say "I believe" even in the moment of impending destruction one was not really a believer. See "In Dust and Ashes" in *The Inner Eye*, Vol. II, selected essays by Hayim Greenberg, ed. Shlomo Katz (New York: Jewish Frontier Publishing Association, 1964).
7. Karl Shapiro, "The Synagogue," in *Poems, 1940–1953* (New York: Random House, 1953).
8. Franz Rosenzweig, *Briefe* (Berlin: Schocken Verlag, 1935), p. 201.

minute historical facts. But on the whole these matters remained for me on the periphery of my interest; I had neither
a strong intellectual drive in any particular direction nor a
deep commitment to any cause. I could with equal ease have
turned to any number of life pursuits; I considered mathe-
matics and architecture, and ended up by going to law
school. I found a judicial career vaguely attractive and sometimes thought in my political naïveté that the diplomatic
service might suit me well.

WHEN THE SWASTIKAS GREW LARGER

Anti-Semitism had been with me from early childhood.
It seemed to be a normal by-product of German public life.
In high school my class mates, most of them older than I,
had little use for the five Jewish boys in their midst. Kicks
and slaps and occasional beatings were my regular fare,
and it was not until my last year that I felt big enough to
reciprocate. All five of us were schooled in an inconspic-
uous but real, long-term endurance contest. Perhaps the
need for some physical achievement, added to my active
nature, made me turn to athletics as my one major interest.
At sixteen a cousin gave me a tennis racket and thereby
an entrance into a new world, with coaches and tourna-
ments, travel, and what I thought was glamor. During the
winter I played soccer and for one year played on a major league team. My teammates were workmen for whom
I was an oddity: a Jewish intellectual who came from a
different world. They accepted me but I was not one of
them. Still, I found more kindness and plain humanity
there than I did at the university where scar-faced frater-
nity students sported swastikas which seemed to get larger
and more numerous year after year.

I joined a Social-Democratic student organization, having
intuitively resisted the entreaties of fraternal groups. In

Heidelberg where I spent a little time in 1931 we were embroiled in minor street clashes with Nazis, but I don't believe this touched me deeply. I think now, in looking back, that I despised them more than I feared or hated them. I still remember the day when during my last high school year my desk neighbor who had sat with me for six years appeared one day with the hooked cross pinned to his lapel. He had joined the S.A. I never spoke to him again, though we sat side by side until the day we graduated.

This was the way many of us Jews lived in those days. The clouds were gathering, but they had always been there. Hitler was threatening, but threats were not new to us. We all remembered the Great War and the revolution and the days of inflation. Now it was unemployment and depression which added fresh explosives to an already highly volatile society. While the tensions increased all about us, we managed somehow to lead an isolated middle-class life at home. At the university we were thrust among the German upper class and in turn isolated by them because we were Jews. I attended a few necessary law seminars and otherwise played soccer, tennis, and chess while Germany was beginning to burn. If I was afraid it was the dull fear which never left the Jew in Germany, and if I was rejected I would manage to live my own life among my own people.

At that time I came across a passage in a book by Jakob Wassermann. After all these years it still stands out clearly in my mind.

It is in vain to adjure the nation of poets and thinkers in the name of its poets and thinkers. Every prejudice that one believed overcome brings forth a thousand new maggots like a carcass.

It is in vain to present the right cheek after the left one has been struck. It does not make them hesitant in the least, it does not touch them, it does not disarm them: they will strike the right cheek also.

It is in vain to cast words of reason into the raving tumult of words. They say: "What, he dares to make a sound? Shut up his face!"

It is in vain to be an example. They say: "We know nothing, we have seen nothing, we have heard nothing."

It is in vain to seek obscurity. They say: "The coward! His bad conscience forces him to hide away."

It is in vain to go among them and offer them one's hand. They say: "How dare he with his Jewish pushiness!"

It is in vain to be loyal to them, either as a fellow fighter, or as a fellow citizen. They say: "He is like Protheus, he can do anything."

It is in vain to help them break the chains of slavery from their arms. They say: "He has probably made his profit doing so."

It is in vain to neutralize the poison. They brew it afresh.

It is in vain to live for them or to die for them. They say: "He is a Jew."[1]

I had not as yet been as deeply disillusioned as Wassermann, but I was on my way. Hitler came to power as I prepared for my finals in law school, and the German people affirmed his rule at the polls while I was writing my exams. When I had finished and was graduated I was also finished with my law career. The Nazis no longer permitted a Jew in the legal profession. My house of pretenses and illusions had collapsed. Rome was burning and I had no place to turn.

I considered going abroad "until the madness blew over," as we were sure it would. I did not then consider emigration. My family's roots were sunk deep into the land and its culture, even though we had never been truly a part of its people. It was a strange contradiction; seen in retrospect it seems unbelievably shortsighted. Father was a historian, yet he too did not see the contradiction. He believed in progress and slow evolution. He had no precedent for what was yet to come.

We considered England as a possible place where I would continue my studies. Nothing came of it because we realized that the English legal system was incompatible with the Latin foundation of German law. I did not want to start all over again and decided I would temporize at home.

MY WAY BACK TO SINAI

It was at the end of 1933 that I first entered the doors of the Hochschule für die Wissenschaft des Judentums, the liberal Jewish theological seminary in Berlin. I went there because it seemed the logical thing to do: the Nazis held us up to ignominy and persecuted us for being Jews. At least I wanted to know what it truly meant to be a Jew if I was made to suffer for it. Synagogues began to fill up, Jewish education courses were now oversubscribed. A young student, Abraham Joshua Heschel, helped me with my Hebrew studies and I enjoyed the few courses I took. I had no professional intentions when I started. It was purely a holding operation. I filled my time with worthwhile pursuits. It was an intellectual pastime. I would still some day return to the law, or so I thought.

I had not reckoned with the inexorable progress of events, and even less had I foreseen that once I came face to face with the real content of my heritage I would be completely captivated by it. The more I learned the more I wanted to learn, and suddenly prayer too assumed a new dimension.

The man who opened the doors to spiritual insight, for me was Leo Baeck. His course was homiletics, but it was really a living inquiry into the soul of man, biblical and modern, of ways to reach out to another heart, of ways to put into words what the mind had grasped. From him I learned how to read in depth, and in the reading, listen to what the author tried to say; from him also I learned to respect the unknown audience whom some day I would address. "When you stand on pulpit or platform," he once told us, "don't attempt to tell your listeners everything about the subject. They are thinking people, don't demean them by denying them the opportunity to think for themselves. The power of your lecture should begin when you are finished speaking." On another occasion he warned us: "When you quote the Bible, don't weight the citation down with superfluous encomia. Don't say: 'As Isaiah said so beautifully . . . ,' or 'As Amos said with such perception . . . ,' just quote and let the author speak for himself. You will do him more justice that way."

Baeck was the man whom German Jewry chose as its head during the difficult years that broke upon us; he was the one who refused to leave the country because he deemed it his duty to stay with his people until the bitter end. The story of his heroism and how he survived the concentration camp has often been told. To me he was teacher and spiritual catalyst. His personal presence had a far greater influence on me than his writings. And he was the one who one day called five of us into his study and showed us a letter from America. Hebrew Union College in Cincinnati had invited us to cross the ocean.

It was little more than a year since I had begun to visit the Hochschule, but by this time my mind was made up: I would be a rabbi. I don't know when I reached the decision; in fact, I don't think I ever decided in any single moment that this would be my way. It unfolded itself, first as possibility, then as certainty. The rabbinate was my complete identification with my people, it was my way back to Sinai.

At first, God was not a conscious factor in this choice, or perhaps I should say that I gave my relationship to Him little thought. As always I went to the synagogue with regularity; I knew the prayers by heart and said them sincerely, but there was no personal relationship. I came to God through my people, their thoughts, their hopes, their doubts, their poetry, and their suffering. It was a slow process which included the early years of my rabbinate.

THE ROLE OF THE RABBI

This may seem puzzling to the reader. How can one be a rabbi without a sure belief? How can a rabbi lead his congregation in prayers if he himself is uncertain of the ground on which he stands?

The answer to this apparent contradiction has to do with the nature of the rabbinical profession. The rabbi is potentially but not necessarily a *religious* leader in the narrow sense of the word. He is not an officiating priest; there are no sacraments in Judaism. There is not a single act of worship, not a single *mitzvah*, not a single milestone in Jewish life which requires the presence or assistance of a rabbi. Any knowledgeable Jewish adult can lead the congregation at prayers and read from Torah and prophets, and in the traditionalist synagogues the priestly blessing is precisely what it says: a benediction spoken not by rabbis but by descendants of the old priestly family of Aaron. Rabbis are required neither for circumcisions (they are rarely present on such occasions; a professional circumciser usually performs the *mitzvah*), nor at Bar Mitzvahs, nor at funerals, nor at weddings (the rabbi's participation may be required by state ordinance; in Jewish tradition only two witnesses are required to be present when the groom places the ring on the finger of his bride). In the formal religious drama of the individual Jew or the synagogue there is no indigenous place for the rabbi.

His place is primarily that of teacher and, secondarily, of judge. The latter is prominent in today's Israel because the state has yielded the determination of Jewish personal status questions to the rabbinate. But everywhere and always the rabbi is or ought to be a devoted student of three thousand years of Jewish teachings and by his knowledge become a guarantor of Jewish spiritual survival. Modern congregational life, especially in the Dispersion, has blurred this function of the rabbi by comparing him to Christian ministers with their sacramental and worship functions. It has made him in part pastor and temple administrator, preacher and worship conductor. Now the rabbi seems more like a clergyman, a "man of the cloth," a "man of God." It is assumed that like his Christian colleague he "is called" to his profession.

The comparison is faulty. A rabbi's fundamental commitment is to his people and its heritage. His worship will consist of study as well as prayer, but since in this latter capacity he is not really in a privileged position, it does not distinguish him nor determine his career. In the past the existence, personal nature, and omnipotence of God were rarely put in question, and consequently a rabbi's fitness was determined by his learning and personality, not by the specificities of his theology. Despite the changing position of the rabbinate this traditional non-theological orientation is still in evidence.

I will not debate here the question whether a rabbi can be an "atheist" as one practitioner seems to believe. What is an atheist in one man's book is a believer in another's. The fact that a congregation can defend its spiritual leader's right to call himself by such an ascription is indication enough that in truth the rabbi's theological convictions appear to them to be marginal to his service. No rabbinical school except an Orthodox one is likely to inquire into a man's belief. A British chief rabbi declaring a colleague unfit to head an Orthodox congregation because he expressed certain progressive *opinions* raised a storm of protest around the world. It was the man's practice, not his thoughts, which should have been at issue, it was claimed. Heresy trials are repugnant to Jews, and our history has been nearly free of such inquisitional exercises. Even the famous expulsion of Baruch Spinoza from the Amsterdam community was political rather than theological.[2]

It should therefore not be surprising that while theological schools encourage the practice of prayer, they do not treat it as a spiritual art. The American Reform seminary has no formal course in theology, and among the professors as well as the students there are probably as many religious humanists as there are theists. No wonder that future rabbis are taught only the how of prayer, but not how to pray.

It was certainly that way when I arrived at Hebrew Union College in 1935. Strange as it may seem, it was the largely non-theological attitude of faculty and student body that brought me face to face with my first serious decisions. When we five newcomers, joined by a few Americans, began to practice our habit of daily prayers and devotions at meal time, the majority of the student body treated us with amused detachment. *Nolente volente* I became a defender of the Covenant of Israel and of all places, at a rabbinical seminary! (I fear that my own insecurity in this new physical and spiritual environment, reinforced by a tendency toward inflated self-esteem, rendered me a less than effective advocate. It would not have been easy in any case, not for anyone.)

The advance of Hitlerism, the continuing economic depression and the difficult plight of our people in Palestine, all these made concern for theological foundations a less than urgent matter among my friends. Where was the God of history? Did He hide? Was He in self-imposed eclipse? Why drive oneself to spiritual frustration and possible immobility when the world needed men of deed and courage? Bread lines had to be fed; strikes had to be won; the greatest fear, Roosevelt had said, was fear itself, and rabbis would be among the leaders of a new economic and intellectual deal. Zion had to be redeemed, Jews had to be saved. Was this a time for prayer or for performance?

WHERE NOW WAS GOD?

By long habit and by nature my lot fell with the "doers." But the question of God would not be stilled. I was a stranger in a strange land, and I began to search for more permanent anchorage. My vague though wholehearted acceptance of purpose in the world and man's possibility of relating meaningfully to this purpose began to sharpen its focus. The questions of congregants in my first congregation, the accusations speaking from the tortured hearts of parents who had lost a child, confronted me with their insistence and complexity.

The outbreak of the war in Europe coincided with the beginning of my congregational service. School was behind me, the law all but forgotten; a new continent with its millions of souls was waiting, and Hitler was at war. It was to be, in many unimaginably gruesome ways, the turning point for the world. It proved to be so also for me, one man whose life had been snatched from the jaws of destruction.

I still have the sermons I preached in those days. They were the impetuous and often all-too-limited outpourings of a young man who wanted the world to save itself. As the days passed, the direction of my pleading changed subtly yet irrevocably. There was an inward turn, even in the titles I then so laboriously fashioned to reveal my intentions. "Where Now Is God?" I asked one Sabbath; "The Debacle of Action" was the subject for another week. Action for its own sake had been the hallmark of my nature and perhaps of mankind too; but in the end action without inner purpose would be as fruitless as peace for the sake of peace. I did not fully realize then how much I wrote and preached to and for myself. (It is no different now, nor do I think it can be different. One speaks and does not know who listens and who, among the listeners, will truly hear.) My wife, to whom I invariably read my first drafts and who helped me shape my disquisitions into understandable and passable English, frequently asked me after listening patiently to my tortured words: "What do you *really* want to say?"—and I would start all over again. What did I really want to say?

As the battle wore on and I became an active partner to it, as I sat with soldiers in the fox holes and smelled the stench of burning flesh, as death threatened and stretched out its hands, my vision became clearer. Unknowingly I prepared myself for the visit to Hell. In Nordhausen concentration camp, upon which we came in the spring of 1945, more than two thousand dead lay unburied in the streets, the ovens were still smoldering, and the few survivors in their striped uniforms of starvation could hardly stir amid the corpses. Where now was the God of the Covenant? I asked the question and uncertainly limned the answer.

Out of the contradictions of my own soul rose the belief that this very tension was part of the world's essence. It was a thought embraced and explored before; to me it now became more than thought: it became my visible road to God.

I beheld the world sustained in the tension of opposites. There is no life without death, no good without evil, no order without disorder. Fear and confidence, joy and sorrow, love and hate, kindness and cruelty dwell inseparably side by side. Creation is the process which makes this spectrum real, from microcosm to macrocosm. And God to me became He who holds this impossible structure in possible balance and who, for me, provides the opportunity to transcend my own contradictions and consciously avail myself of freedom's choices. I do not know what freedom there is for the rest of His vast creation; but I know that, in however narrow limits, it does exist for me.

With my people's voice I say "Hear O Israel, the Lord our God, the Lord is One," and I affirm His oneness, the orderliness of the universe, the possibility of law. At the same time I also say "our God"—and with the possessive pronoun affirm the possibility of individuation. Israel sought and seeks Him in its special way, and I in turn strive to make Him my own God, even as Abraham, Isaac, and Jacob did in their ways.

How shall I speak of what is most intimate? In the process of telling about it its intimacy and thereby part of its pulsating power are lost. How do I communicate adequately my sense of relatedness, of rootedness, of confidence, of belonging? It is clearly and admittedly utterly personal, and it is in this way that I can speak of a personal God. For personality and individuality are creation's final hallmarks, the climax of the evolutionary process. To know that I can realize myself as a person, and know it at the core of my being, gives "personality" to the power that makes this possible. "In the depth of the human soul lives and grows that which is personal; before it, before the I stands the eternal God, who thereby is the near, personal God."[3]

This knowledge provides my ground for prayer. Have my petitions been "answered"? I do not know, for when answers to intellectual or emotional requirements are forthcoming I am not always sure of their origin. But then again, when I am alone in the world, in hours of reflection, in moments of deep crisis, I am able to transcend my loneliness if not my aloneness. Because there is caring in the world, I can care; because there is love in the world, I can love.

Admittedly, the prayers I share with my congregation do

not always meet the needs of my heart nor do they satisfy my intellectual apprehension of God and His worship. I say them because so far they are the only way my people can pray together, and by long association they open to me multitudinous perspectives in time and depth. If I allow myself to be open and accessible prayer becomes a personal reality. At times God is literally "there"; at times my people, and at times I myself stand like a forbidding wall to keep Him out. Reflection in the midst of the crowd is a difficult art, even though the very presence of the many serves, as it does so often, as an incentive opportunity for prayer. In the act of congregational worship the contradictory nature even of our approach to God is starkly revealed. I do not know of His withdrawal; I know of mine.

As I look across the years of my life I sometimes feel that of the many unlikely tasks laid at my door, this personal testimony is not the least. To open the guarded house of my soul is hard, harder than I thought.

God to me is not the almost human, fatherly, benevolent, yet suprahuman creature who was so simply real to my forebears, the One who wrote their deeds into His book of life and weighed them in the scale, who punished the wicked and rewarded the righteous. To me He is the one who by His being makes it possible for me and for others to overcome the contradictions of creation and, in the human realm, of good and evil. "In all this contradiction," said Baeck, "unity remains, the oneness of God in all its contrasts. Hence the oneness of life, its sense and value, answer and certainty."[4] Neither good nor evil in themselves nor both together would describe His nature, but rather are they built into the structure of man's existence. The author of the Book of Job, in the heavenly setting of his introduction, has God Himself provide for the possibility of evil. He "permits" Satan to test the saint. And for Job He prepares the opportunity to transcend the limits of his human sense of right and wrong by placing his trust in the One beyond himself. God makes goodness real, man however must realize and actualize it; without it, God's potential, so to speak, remains itself unrealized. Alas, man's choices are often limited, and circumstances may reduce them to the vanishing point. At the point of death one does not always have a choice of how to meet the final moment. Freedom's opportunities, too, are uncertain.

IN FINDING MY PEOPLE, I FOUND HIM

Standing at the graves of so many, contemplating the unknown burial places of uncounted millions, I learned less about God than about man. I know now that man is "evil from his youth"—but yet is more than evil. I have seen him at his murderous worst and his heroic best. Man like the universe is both cruel and kind; when he is cruel none surpasses him in viciousness, when he is kind none equals him in love. The presence of God assures that love and justice may become real. This is His goodness and this is why we can call Him the Righteous Judge. We say "Our Father, our King" because we acknowledge that we have a relation to His being; we speak in personal pronouns because our souls are involved. He is a "personal God" for He relates to me, and I to His being. I am a person because there is God.

And there is The Presence. How to describe the experience? Most often it comes to me when I seek the company of the few who say their prayers at the daily worship service. As often as possible I seek these moments which, though outwardly the quiet anchor point of the waning day, are potentially astir with deep excitement. At times, what happens is simple, direct, and unmistakable. A different sense of reality descends on me. I hardly hear the words read or sung, and then a faintly trembling insight—a Yes, a reassurance, an opening, a widening of sense. How long? The people rise and I rise with them; the Ark is opened and slowly I drift back to sounds and shadings. It is over, and yet it is not gone. Something remains: a new knowing of what I must do, a prayer actualized. Is this command? For me it is.

More I cannot say except that in this living relationship I find my humanity validated. I am sure about the reality of moral goals, of meaning in creation, of purpose in evolution. I am less sure about my immediate goals than I am about direction and reach. I am less sure about my every step than about the need to climb. I am sure about the search for I have found, and having found about the need to search, find again and again.

Therefore my wonder and my doubt are never ended. I behold suffering and torture, the mangled bodies of innocent victims, of nature's heedlessness and man's carelessness or homicidal tendencies. I do not know why one dies and another survives, why one is born to idiocy and another to genius. I do not know whether God's hiddenness is necessary so that man may turn freely to him. This is what Rosenzweig believed, that God makes it difficult or even impossible for man to believe in Him, so that man may have the opportunity to believe truly, that is, to trust out of his own will and freedom.[5]

I have learned to live with partial answers even in the realm of faith. For me, belief is not congruous with total knowledge and unquestioned certainties. I do not know how to answer the question of the six million murdered ones, although I feel it is forever directed to me who remains to contemplate their fate. How does the presence of God relate to His chosen people at the hell gates of Auschwitz? I do not know, though I marvel at the possibility of men affirming Him even in the throes of that death.

For this they did. Their affirmations were doubtlessly less poetic than Yossel Rakover's last testament though in no wise less real. How many of them must have said in their hearts: "I die peacefully, but not complacently; persecuted but not enslaved; embittered but not cynical; a believer but not a supplicant; a lover of God but no blind amen-sayer of His. I have followed Him even when He has repulsed me. I have followed His Commandments even when He castigated me for it; I have loved Him even when He has hurled me to the earth, tortured me to death, made me an object of shame and ridicule.

"And these are my last words to you, my wrathful God: nothing will avail You in the least. You have done everything to make me lose my faith in You, but I die exactly as I have lived, crying: 'Hear O Israel, the Lord our God, the Lord is One.'"[6]

What made a Jew, hiding for years in an underground bunker in Cologne, write these words on the walls of his lightless dungeon: "I believe in the sun even when it is not shining; I believe in love even when I do not feel it; I believe in God even when He is silent"?

What made Jews sing the ancient words coined by Maimonides eight hundred years ago, and now thrust forth into the sterile air of burning furnaces with a melody that tore the soul loose from its earthly moorings and made it soar in faith? "I believe with perfect faith that my Redeemer cometh," they chanted, "and even though He be delayed, yet will I believe."

"Yet will I believe"—they said it and I repeat it. Yet will I believe that there is purpose to our striving, that death is overcome by daring faith and deeds of righteousness, that His people still have their task and their place.

> Our name is yet the identity of God
> That storms the falling altar of the world.[7]

The world may be unconcerned about our fate; we will, we must be concerned. I will be, this is my life, my way.

I am a Jew. In the uncertain mission of my people I find my own. Judaism is my pathway of truth, "the track of God in the wilderness of oblivion," as Heschel called it. Jews are its chosen watchmen, now and forever. I speak to them and thereby to the world. I care for them and therefore care for man. They form the base of my existence, and because of them all men have a claim on me.

I behold my people's way in time, the unlikely people plodding along its improbable road, and I behold the God of Israel who says "Thou shalt." To turn the ought into an act of will, that is what God asks of us, that is what I hear Him ask of me. For in the end "I will" turns once again into "I must," and thereupon "the song begins again from the beginning."[8]

Why is a Jew? I have only one answer: because there is God. In finding my people, I found Him; in finding Him I found my people's purpose in history. And in this starry coalescence forever shining with uncertain brilliance, I meet all men in common search for large and noble goals.